KU-472-958

MICROWAVE ENTERTAINING

MICROWAVE
ENTERTAINING
MARIE EMMERSON

CONTENTS

This edition first published 1988 by
Hamlyn Publishing Group
Michelin House
81 Fulham Road
London SW3 6RB

© 1986 Hennerwood Publications Limited

ISBN 0 600 55875 4

Printed in Hong Kong

The first domestic microwave cookers in the 1950s were sold as an adjunct to the freezer and were mainly used for thawing and reheating frozen food. Soon, it became apparent that microwave cookers were suitable for various other cooking operations and today, it is accepted that the microwave cooker complements the freezer and the conventional cooker. Certain operations are highly successful, using the microwave cooker alone, whilst others are more satisfactory when another appliance is used as well. Nevertheless, there are some foods and dishes which are best cooked by traditional methods. The recipes in this book have been designed with the texture and look of the food in mind and, where necessary, the conventional cooker has been used as well as the microwave cooker. For example, a small piece of meat can be cooked quickly and taste good when cooked in the microwave cooker but it will lack eye appeal. In such cases the recipe will suggest that the meat be browned under a grill or in a frying pan before or after microwave cooking.

THE BENEFITS OF THE MICROWAVE COOKER

The microwave cooker is an energy efficient appliance; all the energy produced is used to heat and cook the food and is not wasted on heating up containers, oven shelves and so on. This also means that cooking times are often shorter than in conventional cooking.

Because all the cooking is carried out in a confined area there are less smells, and as the inside of the cooker only gets warm rather than hot, food does not 'burn on' as it does in conventional ovens and so cleaning is less arduous. The problem of handling very hot dishes is reduced too, since it is the food which gets really hot, the containers and the inside of the cooker are only warmed by the heat in the food. The microwave cooker is a very versatile appliance because it can be used for thawing frozen food, reheating pre-cooked food and cooking recipes from scratch. There are many other advantages too. Here are just a few:
– Sauces and soups never scorch or burn.
– Vegetables and fruit can be cooked in very little water which means more vivid colours and less nutrient loss.
– 'Steamed' puddings can be cooked without water, eliminating the need to continually top up.
– Fish in particular, but many other foods as well, can be cooked without fat – a bonus to those on special diets.
– Fats can be softened quickly.
– Small quantities of preserves can be cooked without the risk of scorching.
– Individual portions can be cooked quickly and economically, which is a boon for people on their own.

Although the benefits of the microwave cooker far outweigh its disadvantages, it is as well to be aware of its limitations and to know what it cannot do.

The microwave cooker is not suitable for:
– Deep or shallow fat frying.
– Boiling eggs in their shells.
– Cooking foods which rely on heat to hold a rise, such as Yorkshire pudding and hot soufflés.
– Cooking most raw pastries.

ENTERTAINING WITH THE MICROWAVE

Whether your entertaining is formal or informal, whether your guests are expected or unexpected, the microwave cooker will simplify food preparation. Although the recipes in this book are designed for entertaining, it is always advisable to try out a new recipe beforehand on the family. Failing this, cook the dish in advance and freeze it so that it is ready to reheat, which will give you time to check the seasoning and presentation.

Formal Entertaining

When entertaining formally there is usually time to plan the menu, shopping and cooking. The host needs to be well prepared so as not to spend too much time away from the guests. This is when the microwave comes into its own, especially for reheating precooked soups, casseroles and sauces. Bread rolls can be warmed just before serving, and canapés to serve with drinks can be prepared earlier in the day and heated as required. To cut down on reheating time, take food from the freezer early in the day and keep it, covered, in the refrigerator until required. Vegetables, too, can be cooked ahead and, providing the serving dish can be used in a microwave cooker, warmed through just before required. Mousses, cheesecakes and other cold desserts can also be thawed in the microwave if they are not taken from the freezer early enough. However, do remember that the microwave cooker is not an absolute miracle box; so plan ahead and be selective about using your microwave cooker.

Informal Entertaining

At informal parties guests have a tendency to wander into the kitchen, and there are many snacks and nibbles which can be set out so that they can make use of the microwave cooker themselves. Generally speaking, smaller items are most successful, so arrange a selection of individual pizzas, canned drained frankfurters, vol-au-vents, sausage rolls, bread rolls, garlic bread, jacket potatoes and fondue. Mulled wine is a good party drink and it can be made in a large bowl and kept warm, using the lowest position on the cooker, to save the host having to keep an eye on it. Coffee, too, can be made in advance and reheated in cups or mugs when required. The microwave is very useful for smaller parties, but for larger numbers conventional methods of cooking or reheating are more convenient.

WORKING OUT THE RIGHT SETTING

One of the most important points to remember about your microwave cooker is its **Output** or wattage, which indicates the amount of microwave energy available. It is also important to know the meaning of the markings on the **control dial or panel**. When you know these two facts, you can use any microwave recipe from books or magazines with relative ease, and need not stick solely to the manufacturer's handbook.

The Output (wattage)

The output of your microwave cooker may be 400, 500, 600, 650, or 700 watts. This can be checked in the manufacturer's handbook and on the rating plate, a small piece of metal or a label fixed to the back or side of the cooker which also gives its model number.

The recipes in this book have been tested on a 700 watt output cooker so if you have a model with a lower output it may be necessary to increase the cooking times, especially for foods which take a long time to cook. Precise timings cannot be given as much will depend upon the temperature, quantity and density of the food as well as the size, material and shape of the container in which it is cooked. Check the food when it says in the recipe, then continue to check frequently.

The following times are given for general guidance but always keep an eye on the food and refer to the manufacturer's handbook as well. With a 600 watt cooker increase the cooking time by 10-15 seconds for every 1 minute on the recipe; with a 500 watt cooker increase the cooking time by 15-20 seconds for every 1 minute, and with a 400 watt cooker increase the time by 20-25 seconds for every 1 minute.

The Basic Microwave Cooker with a Defrost Setting

A basic microwave cooker has two settings, one for most general cooking operations and one for thawing and slower cooking. This control is generally marked "Defrost". When the cooker is switched on to the main setting, Full 100%, the maximum output of microwave energy is available; on the "Defrost" position the output is automatically reduced. Although the manufacturer may give the output it is easier to know the percentage; on the main setting it will be 100% output and the "Defrost" setting may be 30%. Many of the recipes in this book use the term Defrost (30%). This indicates that if the Defrost setting is 30% then the recipe can be used with the extra time calculated from the paragraph above. However, if the "Defrost" setting is higher or lower than 30%, then the cooking time will vary and this must be taken into account.

The Variable Control Microwave Cooker

This control is simply a method of enabling the user to select more or less microwave energy to suit his or her particular cooking needs. As a dimmer switch gives a choice of lighting levels, so microwave energy can also be adjusted. There is no standardization of settings between models, but the handbook supplied with each individual cooker gives guidance on which setting is best suited for specific cooking operations. Like the Defrost control, the timer is set and the cooker will automatically adjust to the selected cooking level.

To enable more people to use the recipes in this book, only the Full (100%) and Defrost (30%) settings have been used.

A cooker with a variable control may also have a Defrost setting but sometimes the cooker manufacturer will mark the dial or panel with words or figures. It is therefore important to check with the manufacturer's instruction book to establish exactly where the 30% position is on your particular model. Other settings can be used but guidance should be taken from the manufacturer's handbook.

A Guide to Comparative Power Settings

Not all manufacturers use the same names for the variable power settings. The following chart gives some indication of what they may be, but is for guidance only and it is advisable to check your handbook.

1	2	3	4	5	6	7
Keep Warm	Simmer	Stew	Defrost	Bake	Roast	High
Low	Defrost	Med-Low	Medium	High	Med-High	Full
150 watts	200 watts	250 watts	300 watts	400 watts	500 watts	650/700 watts
(25%)	(30%)	(40%)	(50%)	(60%)	(75%)	(100%)

Table by courtesy of The Microwave Association

CONTAINERS

Containers for use in the microwave follow a different set of requirements from those suitable for conventional cookers. Here is a list of what can and cannot be used.

Metal

Metal can cause 'arcing' (i.e. sparking) which can result in the internal walls of a cooker becoming pitted, so unless the manufacturer specifies it, metal in any form should not be used in a microwave. This includes china decorated with metal, and any material which contains metal such as roasting bags with metal ties. Unless the manufacturer recommends it, the use of small pieces of foil or shallow foil containers should not be used.

China, ceramic and oven-to-table

All china, including teapots, is suitable for the microwave, providing it is free of metal and metal decoration, and as long as its handles have not been glued on. The use of antique china should be avoided. Porous pottery is not really suitable for the microwave as the moisture absorbed in the pottery itself heats up, making the container hot, unlike most microwave containers which remain cool. This absorption slows down the cooking by an unknown and variable amount.

Glass

Glass tumblers and small dishes are suitable for the microwave but they should not be used for recipes where the food is likely to reach such a high temperature that the glass may crack; for this reason, food with a high proportion of sugar or fat should not be cooked in a glass container. Never use antique glass or glass with metal decorations in a microwave and never leave a thermometer in a bowl while cooking preserves.

Plastic

Thermoplastic containers including boil-in-the-bag packs, cling film and roasting bags can be used in the microwave. There are also several ranges of special plastic microwave cookware available.

Wood, Baskets and Paper

Wooden utensils and baskets may be placed in the microwave cooker but only for a short time. Baskets which are fastened with wire or staples should not be used. Paper towels, greaseproof paper and cardboard containers can be used in the microwave but avoid those with a wax finish, as the wax may melt from the heat of the food.

Container sizes

Here is a guide to the sizes of the containers used in the recipes in this book. A large bowl has a 3 litre (5¼ pint) capacity; a medium bowl has a 2 litre (3½ pint) capacity and a small bowl a 1 litre (1¾ pint) capacity. A large jug contains 1 litre (1¾ pint) and a small jug contains 0.55 litre (1 pint).

When a dish is to be cooked in a conventional oven or under a grill as well as in the microwave, always check first that the container is suitable.

When a covering is required this may be cling film, a plate or a casserole lid. Where a specific type of cover is required this is stated in the recipe. Should a dish not need covering, but may have a tendency to splash or splatter, place a paper towel over the food. Generally it does not matter what type of utensil is used for stirring, etc., provided that metal utensils are not left in the cooking cavity during the actual cooking.

FREEZING AND THAWING

Freezing

Where a recipe is suitable for freezing this is indicated by an Ⓕ symbol. Should one not be given, the author feels that the dish is better freshly made. However if you wish to freeze a recipe without an Ⓕ symbol this may be possible, but the quality of the finished dish must be judged by the individual. Although it is often felt that making a recipe and freezing it ahead can save time this does not always apply to food cooked in a microwave cooker. There are several recipes in the book which can be made from scratch in the same time, or even in less time, then it takes to thaw and reheat the frozen version. Always compare the original cooking time with the thawing and reheating time before deciding to freeze a dish.

The same principles apply to freezing fresh food whether it is to be cooked in a conventional oven or in a microwave, but remember that if food is frozen in foil or metal trimmed containers they cannot be used in the microwave cooker. All food should be cooled before it is frozen, and suitable wrappings or containers used, and the containers sealed, labelled and dated. If desired (and there is space on the label) thawing instructions may be added to save time later.

Thawing

The thawing times given in this book have all been tested, but they are only approximate as much depends on the quantity of food and the shape, material and size of the containers used. However, it is very important when thawing and heating meat, game or poultry to ensure that the flesh is very hot and not simply warm. This also applies when reheating conventionally. If the output of your cooker is lower than 700 watts it will be necessary to increase the times as explained on page 7.

COOKING INSTRUCTIONS

Sometimes instructions are given which may seem unnecessary, but there are reasons behind them all.

★ Stir liquids. The outer areas of soups, sauces and stews get the most exposure to microwave energy, so stirring means that the liquid will heat more evenly.

★ Rearrange food. Unevenly shaped foods, like fish, may cook more quickly in some parts than others, but by rearranging or turning them over this can be controlled.

★ Turn over large items like joints and poultry. As these foods tend to be irregularly shaped, the microwave exposure varies across the food; turning over means a more even cooking result.

★ Turn around containers. This is particularly beneficial when cooking cakes as it contributes to an even rise.

★ Set aside, covered or leave to stand, covered. After cooking, the food is left to stand for a specific number of minutes. This is not done in order to keep food warm, but because foods continue to cook by conduction after switching off the microwave energy. To avoid dehydration, some foods benefit from being left to stand before serving. This is particularly important with large joints of meat, but also applies to some cakes and puddings.

★ Prick or score any foods with a skin or membrane, such as unpeeled apples, jacket potatoes, whole tomatoes, sausages or egg yolks. This simple precaution prevents the food from bursting.

★ Stand on an upturned plate. This instruction is usually given in recipes for cakes or large joints of meat and helps to cook the centre of the food.

USING THE RECIPES

The recipes in this book have been tested in a cooker with a maximum output of 700 watts. Those with a microwave cooker with a lower wattage may sometimes find it necessary to increase the cooking time slightly (page 7) but before doing so, cook the food for the time given in the recipe. Only then should any additional cooking time be considered.

All the food used in these recipes should be at room temperature, unless otherwise stated. Food straight from the refrigerator or in larger quantities may need a slightly longer cooking time.

The oven temperatures given are for conventional convection ovens. Owners of fan ovens should refer to their cooker manufacturer's temperature chart.

Scallops with Vermouth and Cream Sauce

450 g (1 lb) potatoes, peeled and cut into 2.5 cm (1 inch) cubes
3 tablespoons water
salt
1 garlic clove, peeled and finely chopped
50 g (2 oz) butter
25 g (1 oz) plain flour
150 ml (¼ pint) dry vermouth
1 egg yolk, lightly beaten
8 large scallops, cleaned and sliced
3 tablespoons double cream
freshly ground black pepper
1½ tablespoons tomato purée
sprigs of fresh parsley, to garnish

Preparation time: 20 minutes
Cooking time: 15 minutes
Microwave setting: Full (100%)

1. Place the potatoes, water and salt in a medium bowl and cook, covered, for 8 minutes, stirring once. Cover and set aside.
2. Place the garlic and 25 g (1 oz) of the butter in a medium bowl. Cover and cook for 1 minute or until the butter has melted. Stir in the flour and gradually add the vermouth and cook, uncovered, for 2 minutes.
3. Beat in the egg yolk. Stir in the scallops and cream and season with salt and pepper. Cook, uncovered, for 2 minutes.
4. Rub the potatoes through a sieve and beat in the remaining butter and the tomato purée. Season with salt and pepper. Place the potato in a forcing bag fitted with a large star potato nozzle.
5. Pipe the potato around the edges of four scallop shells and spoon the sauce into the centre. F Cook, uncovered, for 2 minutes to reheat, if necessary. Garnish with sprigs of parsley. Serve as a starter.

F Can be frozen for up to 1 month.
M Microwave on Defrost (30%) for 10 minutes, increase to Full (100%) for 8 minutes or until hot. Rearrange the shells once during both operations.

Fish Terrine

Serves 4-6
50 g (2 oz) butter, cut into pieces
2 garlic cloves, peeled and crushed
25 g (1 oz) plain flour
120 ml (4 fl oz) cold fish stock
50 ml (2 fl oz) double cream
¼ teaspoon anchovy essence
300 g (11 oz) cod fillets, skinned and cut into bite-sized pieces
50 g (2 oz) fresh white breadcrumbs
1 egg (size 1), lightly beaten
175 g (6 oz) crab meat
75 g (3 oz) peeled prawns
1 tablespoon lemon juice
½ teaspoon dried oregano
salt
freshly ground black pepper
To garnish:
fresh prawns
slices of lemon
sprigs of fresh parsley

Preparation time: 15 minutes, plus chilling
Cooking time: 12 minutes
Microwave setting: Full (100%)

1. Place the butter and garlic in a large jug. Cook, uncovered, for 1 minute or until the butter has melted.
2. Stir in the flour, then gradually blend in the cold fish stock, double cream and anchovy essence. Cook for 2 minutes, stirring once.
3. Place the pieces of fish in a small bowl. Cook, covered, for 3 minutes, stirring once.
4. Meanwhile, beat the breadcrumbs into the sauce and then beat in the egg. Gently stir in the crab, prawns, lemon juice, oregano, the cooked fish and the fish liquid and add salt and pepper to taste.
5. Spoon the mixture into a 750 ml (1½ pint) soufflé dish. Cook, covered, for 6 minutes, stirring after 2 and 4 minutes.
6. Remove the dish from the microwave cooker and cover tightly with foil. Set aside to cool, then chill in the refrigerator for several hours until firm.
7. Loosen the edges of the dish and turn out the terrine on to a serving dish. Garnish with fresh prawns, lemon slices and sprigs of parsley and serve with a mixed salad as a main course or by itself as a starter.

From the top: Fish terrine; Scallops with vermouth and cream sauce

MOULES MARINIERE

Serves 2
1.2 litres (2 pints) mussels
1 small onion, peeled and finely chopped
25 g (1 oz) butter
175 ml (6 fl oz) dry white wine
1 shallot, peeled and chopped
2 garlic cloves, peeled and finely chopped
1 tablespoon chopped fresh parsley
salt
freshly ground black pepper

Preparation time: 15 minutes
Cooking time: 10 minutes
Microwave setting: Full (100%)

1. Discard any mussels which are not tightly closed. Brush and wash the shells well to remove any weeds and barnacles and, using a sharp knife, remove the beards. Rinse in plenty of cold water until all the grit is washed away. Set aside.

2. Place the chopped onion and the butter in a large bowl. Cook, covered, for 3 minutes. Stir in the wine, shallot, garlic and parsley and season with salt and pepper. Cook, covered, for 2 minutes.

3. Toss the mussels into the bowl. Cook, covered, for 5 minutes or until the shells open. Toss the mussels again halfway through cooking.

4. Pile the mussels on to two warmed serving dishes. Pour over the cooking liquid and serve immediately with lots of French bread.

PRAWN VOL-AU-VENTS

50 g (2 oz) butter, cut into pieces
50 g (2 oz) plain flour
450 ml (¾ pint) milk
150 ml (¼ pint) single cream
1 egg yolk
salt
freshly ground black pepper
100 g (4 oz) peeled prawns
4 vol-au-vent cases, about 7.5 cm (3 inches) in diameter, cooked
To garnish:
4 whole prawns
4 sprigs fresh parsley

Preparation time: 10 minutes
Cooking time: 8 minutes
Microwave setting: Full (100%)

1. Place the butter in a large jug and cook, uncovered, for 1 minute or until it has melted. Stir in the flour, then gradually stir in the milk and the cream. Cook, uncovered, for 5½ minutes or until thick, stirring every 1 minute.

2. Beat in the egg yolk and season to taste with salt and pepper. ⨍ Stir in the prawns and cook, uncovered, for 1 minute. Keep warm.

3. Arrange the vol-au-vent cases in a circle on a paper towel. Heat, uncovered, for 30 seconds. Using a sharp knife remove the centre lid from each vol-au-vent case and retain. Scrape out the inside pastry and discard.

4. Fill each case with the hot sauce and top with the pastry lids. Garnish each one with a whole prawn and a sprig of parsley and serve hot as a starter.

⨍ Freeze the cream sauce, without the prawns, for up to 3 months.

Ⓜ Microwave the sauce on Full (100%) for 8 minutes or until hot, breaking up and stirring with a fork twice. Beat well, add the prawns and heat for about 1 minute.

PICKLED HERRING, SWEDISH-STYLE

1 kg (2 lb) herrings, filleted and cut into bite-sized pieces
¾ tablespoon salt
2 bay leaves
8 white peppercorns
1 tablespoon fresh dill
600 ml (1 pint) hot water
150 ml (¼ pint) white wine vinegar

Preparation time: 10 minutes, plus chilling
Cooking time: 19 minutes
Microwave setting: Full (100%) and Defrost (30%)

1. Place the herrings, salt, bay leaves, peppercorns, dill, hot water and white wine vinegar in a large bowl. Cook, covered, for 4 minutes.

2. Stir, reduce the setting to Defrost (30%), and cook, covered, for 15 minutes. Stand, covered until cool, then chill in the refrigerator.

3. Spoon the herrings into a shallow serving dish and pour over enough of the cooking liquid to cover. Serve as a starter with dark rye bread and add a green salad for a lunch dish.

From the left: Moules marinière; Pickled herring, Swedish-style

13

BOUILLABAISSE

2 tablespoons olive oil
1 medium onion, peeled and sliced
100 g (4 oz) leeks, trimmed and finely sliced
3 garlic cloves, peeled and crushed
1 sprig fresh fennel
1 sprig fresh thyme
1 sliver fresh orange peel
2 bay leaves
2 small tomatoes, skinned, chopped and seeded
225 g (8 oz) cod fillets, skinned and cut into pieces
225 g (8 oz) monkfish, cut into pieces
600 ml (1 pint) cold water
450 ml (¾ pint) hot fish stock
175 g (6 oz) peeled prawns
175 g (6 oz) mussels, cooked
salt
freshly ground black pepper
½ teaspoon powdered saffron
small slices of hot toast, to serve
Rouille:
1 small red pepper, cored, seeded and chopped
1 garlic clove, peeled and chopped
pinch of powdered saffron
1 egg yolk, beaten
25 g (1 oz) crustless white bread
100-120 ml (3½-4 fl oz) olive oil

Preparation time: 15 minutes
Cooking time: 19 minutes
Microwave setting: Full (100%)

1. Place the oil, onion, leeks, garlic, fennel, thyme and orange peel in a large bowl. Cook, covered, for 8 minutes or until the vegetables are tender.
2. Stir in the bay leaves, tomatoes, cod, monkfish and water. Cook, covered, for 6 minutes.
3. Meanwhile, make the rouille. Using a pestle and mortar, crush the red pepper and garlic to a paste. Add the saffron and salt and pepper to taste. Moisten the bread with a little of the cooking liquid from the bouillabaisse and the egg yolk, then work it into the pepper and garlic mixture until it is thoroughly incorporated. Add the oil a little at a time to begin with, as if making mayonnaise, then as the rouille thickens, pour it in in a thin steady stream. Spoon the rouille into a sauceboat.
4. Stir the hot fish stock, prawns and mussels into the bouillabaisse and season with salt and pepper. Cook, covered, for 5 minutes.
5. Remove the bay leaves and stir in the powdered saffron. Taste the bouillabaisse and adjust the seasoning if necessary, then transfer it to a warm soup tureen.
6. To serve, place a few slices of hot toast in each soup bowl and pour over enough soup to moisten generously, then let guests help themselves to some pieces of fish. Hand the rouille separately.

MACKEREL AND MUSSELS IN CIDER SAUCE

8 mackerel fillets, total weight 1 kg (2¼ lb)
300 ml (½ pint) dry cider
grated rind of 1 lemon
water
25 g (1 oz) butter
25 g (1 oz) plain flour
salt
freshly ground black pepper
1 × 100 g (4 oz) can smoked mussels, drained
chopped fresh parsley, to garnish

Preparation time: 10 minutes, plus marinating
Cooking time: 12-13 minutes
Microwave setting: Full (100%)

CURRIED COD

750 g (1½ lb) cod fillets, skinned and cut into large
pieces
1 garlic clove, peeled and finely chopped
1 small cooking apple, peeled, cored and chopped
1 small carrot, peeled and sliced
1 medium onion, peeled and finely chopped
65 g (2½ oz) butter
1½ tablespoons plain flour
450 g (1 lb) tomatoes, skinned and chopped
2 tablespoons tomato purée
50 ml (2 fl oz) coconut cream
300 ml (½ pint) hot fish stock
1 tablespoon lemon juice
½ teaspoon ground coriander
½ teaspoon ground turmeric
½ teaspoon ground mustard seeds
3 teaspoons mild curry powder
1 tablespoon chutney
40 g (1½ oz) long-grain rice
1 tablespoon chopped fresh coriander, to garnish

Preparation time: 20 minutes
Cooking time: 28½ minutes
Microwave setting: Full (100%)

1. Place the fish in a medium bowl and cook, covered, for
4½ minutes. Set aside.
2. Place the garlic, apple, carrot, onion and butter in a large
bowl. Cover and cook for 6 minutes.
3. Stir in the flour. Gradually stir in the tomatoes, tomato
purée, coconut cream, stock, lemon juice, coriander, turmeric, mustard, curry powder, chutney and rice. Cook,
covered, for 13 minutes, stirring after 6½ minutes.
4. Add the fish and its cooking liquid and cook, covered,
for 5 minutes. Spoon the curry on to a warm serving dish,
garnish with the fresh coriander and serve with sliced
tomatoes, poppadoms and mango chutney.

1. Lay the mackerel fillets, head to tail, in a large shallow
dish. Mix together the cider and lemon rind and pour over
the fish. Leave to marinate for about 3 hours.
2. Pour the marinade into a measuring jug and make up to
300 ml (½ pint) with water.
3. Cover the fish and cook for 7-8 minutes, rearranging
halfway through cooking. Set aside, covered, while
making the sauce.
4. Place the butter in a large jug and cook, uncovered, for 1
minute or until melted. Stir in the flour, then gradually
blend in the marinade. Cook, uncovered, for 2 minutes,
stirring once. Season to taste with salt and pepper.
5. Add the mussels to the sauce and cook for a further 2
minutes, stirring once.
6. Lift the fish on to a warm serving platter, pour over the
sauce and garnish with the chopped parsley. Serve hot
with sauté potatoes and peas.

*From the left: Bouillabaisse; Mackerel and mussels in cider
sauce*

15

SQUID IN TOMATO SAUCE

1 kg (2 lb) squid
1 medium onion, peeled and chopped
25 g (1 oz) butter, cut into pieces
2 garlic cloves, peeled and crushed
25 g (1 oz) plain flour
325 ml (11 fl oz) passata (Italian sieved tomatoes)
2 tablespoons dry vermouth or water
1 tablespoon double or whipping cream
salt
freshly ground black pepper
1 teaspoon caster sugar
1 teaspoon mixed dried herbs
chopped fresh parsley, to garnish

Preparation time: 20 minutes
Cooking time: 40 minutes
Microwave setting: Full (100%) and Defrost (30%)

1. Prepare the squid. Pull the head away from the body. Attached to the head are the entrails. Pull out the transparent bone. Cut the tentacles from the head. Discard the head, entrails and bone and peel the skin from the body and tentacles. Wash the squid in cold water and pat dry, then cut the bodies into rings and chop the tentacles.
2. Place the onion, butter and garlic in a large bowl. Cook, covered, for 5 minutes, stirring once.
3. Stir in the flour. Gradually blend in the passata, dry vermouth and cream. Stir in salt and pepper to taste, the sugar, dried herbs and squid pieces. Cook, covered, for 10 minutes, stirring after 2 and 4 minutes.
4. Stir the squid mixture. Reduce the setting to Defrost (30%) and cook for 25 minutes, stirring halfway through cooking. F Spoon on to a warm serving dish and sprinkle with the chopped parsley. Serve hot with a mixed salad.

F Can be frozen for up to 1 month.
M Cook, covered, on Full (100%) for 20 minutes, breaking up gently with a fork after 10 and 15 minutes.

HADDOCK IN PERNOD SAUCE

4 haddock steaks, total weight 1 kg (2 lb)
300 ml (½ pint) single cream, less 2 tablespoons
2 tablespoons Pernod
salt
freshly ground black pepper
20 g (¾ oz) cornflour
water
sprigs of fresh dill, to garnish

Preparation time: 5 minutes
Cooking time: 14 minutes
Microwave setting: Full (100%)

1. Arrange the haddock steaks in a shallow dish with the thin ends facing the centre. Mix together the cream, Pernod, salt and pepper and pour over the fish. Cook, covered, for 11 minutes or until the fish is opaque and cooked.
2. Remove the fish and place on a warm serving dish.
3. Blend the cornflour with a little water to make a smooth paste and stir into the cream mixture. Pour the cream mixture into a large jug and cook, uncovered, for 3 minutes or until thickened, stirring every 1 minute.
4. Pour the sauce over the fish and garnish with fresh dill. Serve immediately with creamed potatoes, buttered carrots and petit pois.

Variation:
This recipe can also be made with salmon steaks instead of haddock, and whisky can be substituted for the Pernod.

CLAM STUFFED SQUID

Choose squid that are about 15-20 cm (6-8 inches) long for stuffing. Smaller ones are too fragile and liable to burst.

1 kg (2 lb) squid
1 medium onion, peeled and chopped
3 tablespoons olive oil
1 garlic clove, peeled and chopped
50 g (2 oz) fresh white breadcrumbs
1 teaspoon mixed dried herbs
1 × 275 g (10 oz) can baby clams in brine, drained
salt
freshly ground black pepper
300 ml (½ pint) cold fish stock (or use half stock and half dry white wine)
20 g (¾ oz) cornflour
water
1 tablespoon double or whipping cream
chopped fresh parsley, to garnish

Preparation time: 35 minutes
Cooking time: 31 ½ minutes
Microwave setting: Full (100%) and Defrost (30%)

1. Prepare the squid. Pull the head away from the body. Attached to the head are the entrails. Pull out the transparent bone. Cut the tentacles from the head. Discard the head, entrails and bone and peel the skin from the body and tentacles. Wash in cold water and pat dry. Set aside the bodies and chop the tentacles into 1 cm (½ inch) pieces.
2. Purée the onion, oil and garlic in a blender, then pour into a medium bowl. Cook, covered, for 3 minutes. Stir in the breadcrumbs, herbs, chopped tentacles and clams and add salt and pepper to taste. Fill each squid about ¾ full to allow room for the stuffing to swell during cooking.
3. Place the squid in a large bowl and pour over the wine

and stock. Cook, covered, for 10 minutes then stir and reduce the setting to Defrost (30%). Cook, covered, for a further 15 minutes, stirring once.

4. Meanwhile, blend the cornflour with a little water to make a smooth paste. Place the squid on a warm serving dish. Stir the cornflour into the cooking liquid and cook, uncovered, on Full (100%) for 3½ minutes, or until thickened, stirring every 1 minute. Stir in the cream.

5. Pour a little sauce over the squid and garnish with chopped parsley. Serve with boiled rice, spinach and the remaining sauce.

Clockwise from top left: Squid in tomato sauce; Clam stuffed squid; Haddock in Pernod sauce

STUFFED TROUT IN RIESLING SAUCE

200 g (7 oz) mushrooms, chopped
25 g (1 oz) butter
½ teaspoon dried sage
salt
freshly ground black pepper
4 trout, total weight 750 g (1½ lb), cleaned, with heads
left on
150 ml (¼ pint) dry Riesling
4 teaspoons cornflour
150 ml (¼ pint) single cream
2 egg yolks
To garnish:
1-2 mushrooms, sliced
1 stuffed olive, cut into 4 slices

Preparation time: 15 minutes
Cooking time: 19 minutes, plus standing
Microwave setting: Full (100%)

1. Place the mushrooms, butter and sage in a large jug. Cook, covered, for 3 minutes, stirring once. Season with salt and pepper to taste.
2. Stuff each trout with ¼ of the mushroom mixture and place them in a shallow dish. Cook, covered, for 12 minutes, rearranging them once. Set aside to stand, covered, for 5 minutes.
3. Place the wine in a small jug and cook, uncovered, for 2 minutes. Meanwhile, blend the cornflour with the cream.
4. Beat the egg yolks into the wine and then beat in the cream. Cook, uncovered, for 2 minutes or until the sauce is thick, beating every 30 seconds. Season with salt and pepper.
5. Arrange the trout on a warm serving platter. Spoon a little sauce over each one and garnish with a sliced mushroom and place a slice of stuffed olive over the eye of each trout. Serve with buttered boiled potatoes, a green salad and the remaining sauce.

Variation:
For a less rich sauce you can substitute the same quantity of milk for the wine and the cream.

TROUT WITH CASHEW NUTS

4 trout, total weight 750 g (1½ lb), cleaned, with heads
left on
salt
freshly ground black pepper
grated rind of 2 lemons
25 g (1 oz) butter
75 g (3 oz) raw cashew nuts, split
4 small sprigs fresh parsley, to garnish

Preparation time: 10 minutes
Cooking time: 15 minutes, plus standing
Microwave setting: Full (100%) and Conventional hob

1. Sprinkle the inside of each trout with salt, pepper and grated lemon rind and place in a shallow dish. Cook, covered, for 12 minutes, rearranging once. Set aside to stand, covered, for 5 minutes.
2. Meanwhile melt the butter in a frying pan on a conventional hob. Stir in the nuts and cook gently until they are golden brown. Set aside the nuts and keep them warm.
3. Arrange the trout on a warm serving dish. Sprinkle over the nuts and garnish with a sprig of parsley. Serve hot with boiled rice and a mixed salad.

Variation:
If preferred substitute split almonds for the cashew nuts.

MONKFISH, MEDITERRANEAN-STYLE

1 garlic clove, peeled and crushed
½ green pepper, seeded and diced
½ yellow pepper, seeded and diced
1 medium onion, peeled and chopped
350 g (¾ lb) tomatoes, skinned and chopped
150 ml (¼ pint) dry white wine
1 teaspoon dried oregano
2 tablespoons tomato purée
1 teaspoon caster sugar
salt
freshly ground black pepper
2 teaspoons cornflour
3 tablespoons brandy
1 kg (2 lb) monkfish, boned and cut into bite sized pieces
2 tablespoons double or whipping cream

Preparation time: 15 minutes
Cooking time: 21 minutes
Microwave setting: Full (100%)

1. Place the garlic, peppers and onion in a large bowl and cook, covered, for 6 minutes, stirring once. Stir in the tomatoes, wine, oregano, tomato purée and sugar and add salt and pepper to taste. Cover and cook for 4 minutes.
2. Mix the cornflour with the brandy to make a smooth paste. Stir into the sauce and cook, uncovered, for 4 minutes, stirring every 1 minute. Set aside. Ｆ
3. Place the monkfish in a large bowl and cook, covered, for 4 minutes, stirring once. Add the tomato sauce and cook, uncovered, for 3 minutes or until hot.
4. Stir in the cream and pile on to a warm serving dish. Serve hot with boiled rice.

Ｆ The sauce can be frozen for up to 3 months.
Ｍ Microwave the sauce on Full (100%) for 8 minutes or until hot, breaking up and stirring once. Continue from step 3.

Clockwise from top left: Stuffed trout in riesling sauce; Monkfish, Mediterranean-style; Trout with cashew nuts

POACHED TURBOT WITH HOLLANDAISE SAUCE

8 turbot fillets, total weight 1¼ kg (2½ lb)
25 g (1 oz) butter, cut into 4 pieces
salt
freshly ground black pepper
4 stuffed olives, sliced, to garnish
Hollandaise sauce:
2 egg yolks
1 tablespoon lemon juice
100 g (4 oz) butter, cut into 8 pieces
pinch of cayenne pepper
½ teaspoon dry mustard

Preparation time: 20 minutes
Cooking time: 8 minutes
Microwave setting: Full (100%)

1. Remove the skin from the turbot fillets and discard. Dot each fillet with a knob of butter and sprinkle with salt and pepper. Roll up each fillet and secure it with a wooden cocktail stick.
2. Place the fillets in a shallow dish and cook, covered, for 7½ minutes, rearranging once. Set aside the fillets, covered, while making the sauce.
3. Mix together the yolks and lemon juice in a small jug and cook, uncovered, for 30 seconds. Beat the mixture until it is smooth, then beat in the butter, 1 piece at a time. Finally beat in the pepper and the mustard.
4. Lift the fish on to a warm serving dish. Pour over the sauce and garnish with slices of stuffed olive. Serve immediately with parsleyed potatoes and mange-touts.

SALMON STEAKS WITH TOMATO AND WHITE WINE SAUCE

4 salmon steaks, total weight 1 kg (2 lb)
25 g (1 oz) butter
25 g (1 oz) plain flour
150 ml (¼ pint) dry white wine
150 ml (¼ pint) single cream, less 2 tablespoons
2 tablespoons tomato purée
salt
freshly ground black pepper
To garnish:
4 giant prawns
4 sprigs fresh dill

Preparation time: 5 minutes
Cooking time: 12 minutes, plus standing
Microwave setting: Full (100%)

1. Place the salmon steaks in a large shallow dish with their thin ends towards the centre. Cook, covered, for 7 minutes, rearranging once. Set the salmon aside to stand, covered, for 5 minutes.
2. Make the sauce. Place the butter in a large jug. Cook, uncovered, for 1 minute or until it has melted. Stir in the flour, then gradually blend in the wine, cream and tomato purée. Cook, uncovered, for 4 minutes, stirring every 1 minute. Season with salt and pepper. F
3. Place the salmon on a warm serving dish. Spoon over the sauce and garnish with giant prawns and sprigs of dill. Serve with boiled new potatoes and a lettuce and cucumber salad.

Variation:
This dish can be made with cod steaks instead of salmon.

F The sauce can be frozen for up to 3 months.
M To thaw and heat, microwave on Full (100%) for 4 minutes or until hot. Break up with a fork halfway through cooking and whisk well before serving.

SALMON IN ASPIC

Serves 4-6
1×1.5 kg (3 lb) salmon
Aspic jelly:
475 ml (16 fl oz) cold clarified fish stock
1 tablespoon powdered gelatine
2 tablespoons dry sherry
1 tablespoon lemon juice
To garnish:
thinly sliced cucumber
slice of stuffed olive
150 ml (¼ pint) thick mayonnaise

Preparation time: 25 minutes, plus chilling and setting
Cooking time: 18½ minutes, plus standing
Microwave setting: Full (100%)

1. Place the stock in a large jug and cook, uncovered, for 6 minutes or until very hot. Sprinkle over the gelatine and whisk well to dissolve. Cook, uncovered, for 30 seconds then stir in the sherry and lemon juice. Cool until thickened but not set.
2. Cover a large plate with cling film and place the salmon on top. Cover the tail and the front of the head with small smooth pieces of aluminium foil then cook, covered, for 12 minutes, turning once. Stand, covered, for 5 minutes then remove the cover and set aside to cool.
3. When cold, carefully remove the skin making a neat cut along the length of the backbone, across the tail and round the head. Using the blade of the knife, scrape away the shallow layer of brown coloured flesh over the centre of the fish. Gently turn over the salmon and repeat the operation on the other side.
4. To remove the backbone, use a long bladed knife to cut along the backbone of the fish, then turn the knife flat and gently ease the fillet from the bone. Using scissors, cut

through the bone at each end and ease it out, then replace the fillet.
5. Spoon a little thickened aspic jelly over the salmon and leave to set. Arrange cucumber slices over the salmon to represent fish scales and place a slice of stuffed olive over the eye. Spoon over another layer of aspic and leave to set.
6. Pour the remaining jelly into a shallow dish and leave to set, then chop with a sharp knife.
7. Lift the salmon on to a large chilled platter. Garnish with piped mayonnaise, and spoon the remaining aspic around the salmon. Serve with potato and green salads.

Variation:
The aspic jelly can be made with aspic jelly crystals instead of the gelatine powder, adding the sherry and lemon juice for extra flavour if necessary.

From the left: Poached turbot with hollandaise sauce; Salmon steaks with tomato and white wine

SKATE WITH BLACK BUTTER

2 skate wings, total weight about 1 kg (2 lb)
4 tablespoons water
175 g (6 oz) unsalted butter
2 tablespoons white wine vinegar
2 tablespoons chopped fresh parsley

Preparation time: 5 minutes
Cooking time: 9 minutes
Microwave setting: Full (100%) and conventional hob

1. Cut each skate wing into two. Place the skate in a large bowl with the thin ends facing the centre. Add the water. Cook, covered, for 9 minutes, rearranging the skate once.
2. Meanwhile place the butter in a frying pan and cook on a conventional hob until it is brown but not scorched. Stir in the vinegar and parsley.
3. Drain the skate. Pull off the skin and discard. Place the fish on a warm serving platter. Pour over the hot butter and serve immediately with buttered boiled potatoes and green beans or a salad.

SOLE NORMANDE

Do not be tempted to use plastic cocktail sticks instead of wooden ones as they could melt during cooking.

12 sole fillets, skinned, total weight 750 g (1½ lb)
salt
freshly ground black pepper
2 tablespoons chopped fresh parsley
Sauce:
grated rind of 1 lemon
1 garlic clove, peeled and finely chopped
50 g (2 oz) button mushrooms, sliced
25 g (1 oz) butter
50 g (2 oz) peeled prawns
50 g (2 oz) mussels, cooked
2 teaspoons brandy
slices of lemon, to garnish

Preparation time: 20 minutes
Cooking time: 10 minutes
Microwave setting: Full (100%)

1. Season the skinned side of the fillets with salt, pepper and parsley. Roll up with the skinned side inwards and secure with wooden cocktail sticks. [A] Place the fish rolls in a shallow dish and cook, covered, for 6 minutes, rearranging once. Set aside, covered.

2. Place the lemon rind, garlic, button mushrooms and butter in a medium bowl and cook, covered, for 2 minutes. Stir in the prawns and the mussels and cook, covered, for a further 2 minutes.

3. Stir in the brandy and season to taste with salt and pepper. Arrange the sole on a warm serving dish, remove the cocktail sticks and spoon over the sauce. Garnish with slices of lemon and serve with creamed potatoes and fried courgettes or another green vegetable.

[A] The fish rolls can be made up to 8 hours in advance, covered and stored in the refrigerator.

2 medium lobsters, cooked
4 slices white bread, cut into large rounds, crusts removed
165 g (5½ oz) butter
1 tablespoon oil
1½ tablespoons brandy
1½ tablespoons dry sherry
pinch of cayenne pepper
salt
freshly ground black pepper
2 egg yolks (size 1), lightly beaten
150 ml (¼ pint) double cream
To garnish:
small lobster claws
paprika pepper

Preparation time: 1 hour 20 minutes
Cooking time: 10 minutes
Microwave setting: Full (100%), and Conventional hob

1. Remove the heads of the lobsters and discard. Split each lobster in half and remove the intestinal vein, stomach and sac of grit. Pull off the large claws, crack and dice the meat. Remove the meat from the body and dice.

2. Place 100 g (4 oz) of the butter and the oil in a frying pan and melt over a low heat on a conventional hob. Gently fry the bread, then set aside to keep warm.

3. Cut the remaining butter into pieces and place in a medium bowl. Cook, uncovered, for 2 minutes. Stir in the brandy, sherry, cayenne pepper, salt and pepper to taste, and the diced lobster meat. Cook, covered, for 3 minutes, stirring gently after 2 minutes.

4. Mix together the egg yolks and the cream. Gently stir into the lobster mixture. Cook, uncovered, for 1½ minutes or until thick, stirring gently every 30 seconds. Take care not to overheat the mixture.

5. Pile the mixture on to the slices of bread and garnish with the small lobster claws and a sprinkling of paprika. Serve hot with boiled rice and a green salad.

From the left: Sole Normande; Lobster Newburg

HOT GAME TERRINE

225 g (8 oz) cold cooked mixed game (such as pheasant,
quail or hare), finely chopped
50 g (2 oz) cooked ham, chopped
50 g (2 oz) mushrooms, finely chopped
2 garlic cloves, peeled and crushed
1 teaspoon mixed dried herbs
salt
freshly ground black pepper
2 eggs, lightly beaten
To garnish:
sprigs of watercress
tomato slices

Preparation time: 10 minutes
Cooking time: 5-6 minutes
Microwave setting: Full (100%)

1. Mix the chopped game, ham, mushrooms, garlic and
herbs in a bowl. Season to taste with salt and pepper and
bind together with the beaten eggs.
2. Place a tall straight-sided glass in the centre of a 16 cm
(6½ inch) soufflé dish lined with cling film to make a ring
mould. Spoon in the game mixture and spread evenly.
3. Cover and cook for 5-6 minutes. Remove the cover and
the glass then turn out on to a warm serving dish and
remove the cling film. Garnish with sprigs of watercress
and tomato slices. Serve as a starter with hot toast.

COCK-A-LEEKIE

1 garlic clove, peeled and crushed
750 g (1½ lb) leeks, trimmed and thinly sliced
3 tablespoons water
1 × 1½ kg (3 lb) chicken, cut into 8 pieces
900 ml (1½ pints) hot chicken stock
1 bouquet garni
salt
freshly ground black pepper

Preparation time: 20 minutes
Cooking time: 51 minutes
Microwave setting: Full (100%) and Defrost (30%)

1. Place the garlic, leeks and water in a large bowl and
cook, covered, for 8 minutes, stirring once.
2. Add the chicken and cook, covered, for a further 8
minutes. Stir in the hot stock, bouquet garni and salt and
pepper to taste. Cook, covered, for 5 minutes then reduce
to Defrost (30%). Cook for 30 minutes or until the chicken
is tender, stirring after 15 minutes.

3. Remove the bouquet garni, then lift out the chicken
pieces and pull off the skin. Cut the flesh into large pieces
and return them to the soup, then taste and adjust the
seasoning. Pour the soup into four warm bowls and serve
as a substantial starter or as a supper dish.

CHICKEN LIVER MOUSSE

Serves 4-6
225 g (8 oz) chicken livers
1 garlic clove, crushed
1 tablespoon chopped fresh parsley
salt
freshly ground black pepper
25 g (1 oz) butter
25 g (1 oz) plain flour
200 ml (7 fl oz) milk
2 eggs, lightly beaten
2 teaspoons powdered gelatine
85 ml (3 fl oz) double or whipping cream
To garnish:
sprigs of fresh parsley
slices of lemon

Preparation time: 10 minutes, plus cooling and chilling
Cooking time: 9 minutes
Microwave setting: Full (100%)

1. Place the chicken livers, garlic, parsley and salt and
pepper to taste in a medium bowl and cook, covered, for 4
minutes, stirring after 2 minutes. Set aside.
2. Place the butter in a large jug and cook, uncovered, for 1
minute or until melted. Stir in the flour, then the milk and
cook, uncovered, for 2½ minutes, stirring every 1 minute.
Beat in the eggs and cook, uncovered, for 1½ minutes,
beating every 30 seconds. Add the gelatine to the hot
mixture and stir until dissolved.
3. Place the sauce and chicken liver mixture in a liquidizer
or food processor and purée until smooth. Season with
salt and pepper and set aside to cool, stirring occasionally.
4. Whip the cream until it holds stiff peaks and fold it into
the chicken liver purée. Spoon into a cling film lined
900 ml (1½ pints) loaf dish. Cover and chill overnight in
the refrigerator.
5. Turn out the mousse on to a chilled plate, remove the
cling film and garnish with parsley and lemon slices. Serve
as a starter with hot toast.

From the top: Chicken liver mousse; Hot game terrine

CHICKEN WITH SPICY SAUSAGE

Serves 4-6
1 medium onion, peeled and finely chopped
2 garlic cloves, peeled and crushed
2 green peppers, seeded and finely sliced
1 × 1½ kg (3 lb) chicken, cut into 8 pieces
4 tomatoes, skinned and chopped
1 tablespoon tomato purée
150 ml (¼ pint) hot chicken stock
120 ml (4 fl oz) dry white wine
salt
freshly ground black pepper
3 teaspoons cornflour
water
100 g (4 oz) Polish kabanos sausage, sliced

Preparation time: 20 minutes
Cooking time: 58 minutes
Microwave setting: Full (100%)

1. Place the onion, garlic and green peppers in a large bowl and cook, covered, for 10 minutes, stirring after 5 minutes.
2. Stir in the chicken, tomatoes, tomato purée, stock, wine and salt and pepper to taste. Cook, covered, for 45 minutes or until tender, stirring occasionally.
3. Remove the chicken and vegetables, place on a warm serving dish and keep warm.
4. Blend the cornflour with a little water to make a smooth paste and stir into the sauce with the sausages. Cook, uncovered, for 3 minutes, stirring every 1 minute, until thickened. Pour the sauce over the chicken and vegetables. Serve hot with boiled noodles.

TURKEY AND VEGETABLE SOUP

25 g (1 oz) butter
1 medium onion, peeled and chopped
225 g (8 oz) carrots, peeled and finely sliced
100 g (4 oz) leeks, white part only, sliced
100 g (4 oz) potato, peeled and sliced
1 tablespoon tomato purée
1 teaspoon mixed dried herbs
900 ml (1½ pints) hot turkey or chicken stock
350 g (12 oz) cooked turkey meat, cut into bite-sized pieces
salt
freshly ground black pepper

Preparation time: 15 minutes
Cooking time: 24 minutes
Microwave setting: Full (100%)

1. Place the butter, onion, carrots, leeks, potato, tomato purée and herbs into a large bowl and cook, covered, for 10 minutes, stirring once.
2. Pour the hot stock and vegetables into a liquidizer or food processor. Purée until smooth then return the mixture to the bowl.
3. Stir in the turkey meat and season with salt and pepper to taste. Cook, uncovered, for 14 minutes, stirring occasionally. ⅀ Pour into four warm serving bowls and serve hot with thick slices of French bread.

⅀ Can be frozen for up to 3 months.
Ⓜ Microwave, uncovered, on Full (100%) for 25 minutes or until hot, breaking up and stirring after 10 and 15 minutes.

CHICKEN WATERZOOI

This soup is a great favourite in Holland and Belgium.
Another version is made with freshwater fish.
Serves 4-6
1 × 1½ kg (3 lb) chicken
1 leek, white part only, sliced
1 medium onion, peeled and chopped
4 sticks celery, chopped
2 sprigs fresh parsley
2 garlic cloves, crushed
1 carrot, chopped
¼ teaspoon grated nutmeg
¼ teaspoon dried thyme
3 cloves
salt
freshly ground black pepper
about 1.2 litres (2 pints) hot chicken stock
1 lemon, thinly sliced
1 tablespoon chopped fresh parsley
4 egg yolks, beaten with 4 tablespoons double cream

Preparation time: 15 minutes
Cooking time: 55 minutes
Microwave setting: Full (100%) and Defrost (30%), and Conventional hob

1. Place the chicken, breast side down, in a large bowl and cook, covered, for 15 minutes. Mix together the leek, onion, celery, sprigs of parsley, garlic, carrot, nutmeg, thyme, cloves and salt and pepper to taste. Place around the chicken and pour over sufficient stock to almost cover the chicken.
2. Cook, covered, for 5 minutes then reduce the setting to Defrost (30%) and cook for a further 30 minutes.
3. Remove the chicken from the stock and, when it is cool enough to handle, take the flesh from the bones in large pieces, discarding the skin. Keep the chicken warm.
4. Strain 750 ml (1¼ pints) of the stock into a clean saucepan, ⅀ add the lemon slices and chopped parsley and heat on a conventional hob until almost boiling.
5. Stir a little hot stock into the egg yolk mixture, then pour

back into the saucepan. Continue stirring over a low heat until the sauce has thickened slightly. (Do not allow it to boil.) Remove from the heat and stir in the chicken pieces. Pour into a heated tureen and serve immediately.

Ⓕ Add the chicken pieces to the strained stock and freeze for up to 3 months.
Ⓜ Microwave on Full (100%) for about 20 minutes, stirring twice, then continue from step 4.

Clockwise from top left: Chicken with spicy sausage; Chicken waterzooi; Turkey and vegetable soup

CHICKEN CHAUDFROID

1 × 1½ kg (3 lb) oven ready chicken
Chaudfroid sauce:
1 small carrot, peeled
1 small celery stick, halved
1 small onion, quartered
8 black peppercorns
600 ml (1 pint) milk
600 ml (1 pint) cold water
25 g (1 oz) aspic jelly powder
50 g (2 oz) butter
50 g (2 oz) plain flour
salt
ground white pepper
1 teaspoon powdered gelatine
4 tablespoons double cream
To garnish:
3 small peppers (green, yellow and red)
sprigs of fresh parsley

Preparation time: 35 minutes, plus cooling and chilling
Cooking time: 32 minutes, plus standing
Microwave setting: Full (100%)

1. Place the chicken, breast side down, in a shallow container and cook, uncovered, for 10 minutes. Turn over and cook for 11 minutes, then wrap tightly in foil and stand for 20 minutes. Remove the foil, and carefully take off the skin. Cut off the wings and parson's nose and discard. Remove the trussing string when the chicken is cool.
2. Place the carrot, celery, onion, peppercorns and milk in a large jug and cook, uncovered, for 4 minutes. Set aside to infuse for 15 minutes, then discard the vegetables.
3. Place 300 ml (½ pint) of the cold water in a large jug and cook, uncovered, for 3½ minutes. Add the aspic jelly powder and stir until dissolved. Stir in the remaining water and stand the jug in a bowl of hot water to prevent the jelly from setting.
4. Place the butter in a large jug and cook, uncovered, for 1 minute or until melted. Stir in the flour, then the strained milk and salt and pepper to taste. Cook for 2½ minutes, stirring every 1 minute.
5. Sprinkle the gelatine powder over the white sauce and stir well to dissolve. Stir in 150 ml (¼ pint) of the aspic jelly, cool slightly and stir in the cream.
6. Place the chicken on a wire tray over a plate. Then using a large spoon, pour a layer of white sauce over the chicken. Leave to set before applying two more layers of sauce.
7. Cut the peppers into diamond or flower shapes. Arrange the garnish on the chicken and spoon over a layer of aspic jelly. Leave to set and then apply a second layer. Chill in the refrigerator for at least 2 hours until set.
8. Pour the remaining aspic jelly into a shallow dish and chill in the refrigerator until set, then chop roughly.
9. Place the chicken on a chilled oval platter surrounded by the chopped jelly and garnish with parsley.

GRUYERE CHICKEN IN WHITE SAUCE

4 chicken breasts, boned, each about 185 g (6½ oz)
150 ml (¼ pint) single cream
50 ml (2 fl oz) dry white wine
1 teaspoon chopped fresh tarragon
salt
freshly ground black pepper
75 g (3 oz) Gruyère cheese, grated
2 teaspoons cornflour
water
4 sprigs fresh tarragon, to garnish

Preparation time: 10 minutes
Cooking time: 15½-16 minutes
Microwave setting: Full (100%), and Conventional grill

1. Place the chicken breasts in a shallow dish and cook, covered, for 8 minutes. Rearrange the chicken breasts, then prick them with a fork.

2. Pour over the cream, wine and tarragon and season with salt and pepper to taste. Cook, covered, for 6 minutes, turning after 3 minutes.

3. Using a slotted spoon, transfer the chicken breasts to a flameproof serving dish and sprinkle with the cheese. Brown under a preheated conventional grill.

4. Meanwhile, place the cornflour in a small bowl, add a little water and mix to a smooth paste. Stir in the chicken liquid and cook, uncovered, for 1½-2 minutes, stirring every 30 seconds.

5. Pour the sauce around the chicken and garnish with sprigs of tarragon. Serve hot with parsleyed potatoes and buttered courgettes.

CHICKEN GALANTINE

Serves 4-6
50 g (2 oz) fresh white breadcrumbs
25 g (1 oz) hazelnuts, finely chopped
1 teaspoon dried tarragon
1 teaspoon dried thyme
1 teaspoon dried parsley
salt
freshly ground black pepper
350 g (12 oz) pork sausage meat
1 × 1.75 kg (4 lb) chicken, boned
100 g (4 oz) ham, cut into strips
50 g (2 oz) pistachio nuts
6 black olives, stoned and quartered
Aspic jelly:
475 ml (16 fl oz) cold clarified chicken stock
1 tablespoon powdered gelatine
2 tablespoons dry sherry
1 tablespoon lemon juice
3 peppers (red, green and yellow), cut into thin diamond shapes, to garnish

---

Preparation time: 45 minutes, plus cooling and setting
Cooking time: 27 ½ minutes, plus chilling
Microwave setting: Full (100%)

---

1. Mix together the breadcrumbs, hazelnuts, tarragon, thyme and parsley and season with salt and pepper then, using your hands, work in the sausage meat.

2. Put the chicken on a board, skin side down, and smooth the flesh into an even layer.

3. Arrange the ham over the chicken, and sprinkle over the nuts and olives. Form the stuffing into an oblong and place in the centre of the chicken. Tuck in the ends, then fold the sides of the bird over the stuffing to form a neat roll. Check that the roll is not too long to fit into the cooker.

4. Tie the roll very securely with string and use wooden cocktail sticks to secure if necessary. Put the chicken roll, seam side down, in a shallow dish and cook, uncovered, for 21 minutes. Remove the galantine from the microwave and wrap tightly in foil. Place heavy weights on top and leave until cold, then remove the string and cocktail sticks.

5. To make the aspic jelly, place the stock in a large jug and cook, uncovered, for 6 minutes or until very hot. Sprinkle over the gelatine and whisk well to dissolve. Cook, uncovered, for 30 seconds, then stir in the sherry and lemon juice. Set aside until cool and beginning to set.

6. Spoon a layer of aspic over the chicken and leave to set. Spoon over a second layer and when nearly set garnish with green, yellow and red pepper shapes. Spoon over a further layer of aspic and allow to set.

From the left: Chicken chaudfroid; Chicken galantine

TURKEY MARENGO

1 large onion, peeled and chopped
25 g (1 oz) butter
2 garlic cloves, peeled and crushed
4 turkey legs, total weight 1½ kg (3¼ lb)
25 g (1 oz) plain flour
200 ml (7 fl oz) Marsala
150 ml (¼ pint) hot chicken stock
1 teaspoon dried mixed herbs
2 tablespoons tomato purée
350 g (12 oz) tomatoes, skinned and chopped
salt
freshly ground black pepper
175 g (6 oz) button mushrooms

Preparation time: 20 minutes
Cooking time: 1 hour 36 minutes
Microwave setting: Full (100%) and Defrost (30%)

1. Place the onion, butter, garlic and turkey legs in a large bowl and cook, covered, for 15 minutes, rearranging once.
2. Remove the turkey legs and set aside. Stir the flour into the onions with the Marsala, stock, herbs, tomato purée, tomatoes and add salt and pepper to taste. Cook, covered, for 3 minutes. Stir in the mushrooms and cook for a further 3 minutes.
3. Transfer the turkey legs to a large deep casserole and pour over the sauce. Reduce the setting to Defrost (30%) and cook, covered, for 1¼ hours or until the turkey is tender, rearranging several times during cooking. Serve hot with buttered noodles.

CHICKEN WITH GRAPES

4 small pickling onions, peeled
4 chicken breasts, each about 185 g (6½ oz)
50 ml (2 fl oz) dry white wine
50 ml (2 fl oz) hot chicken stock
1 garlic clove, crushed
salt
freshly ground black pepper
2 teaspoons cornflour
water
175 g (6 oz) white grapes, skinned, halved and seeded
1 tablespoon double or whipping cream
sprigs of fresh coriander or parsley, to garnish

Preparation time: 25 minutes
Cooking time: 27½ minutes
Micorwave setting: Full (100%) and Defrost (30%)

1. Place the onions in a medium bowl, arrange the chicken breasts in a single layer over the top and cook, covered, for 5 minutes.
2. Rearrange the chicken, add the wine, stock, garlic and

salt and pepper to taste. Reduce the setting to Defrost (30%) and cook for 20 minutes or until tender, stirring after 10 minutes.
3. Arrange the chicken and onions on a warm serving dish and keep warm.
4. Blend the cornflour with a little water to make a smooth paste and stir into the sauce with the grapes. Cook, uncovered, on Full (100%) for 2½ minutes, stirring every 1 minute.
5. Stir in the cream. Taste and adjust the seasoning, then pour the sauce over the chicken. ⦅F⦆ Garnish and serve hot with duchesse potatoes and broccoli.

⦅F⦆ Can be frozen for up to 3 months.
⦅M⦆ Microwave, covered, on Full (100%) for 20 minutes, gently separating and rearranging after 5 and 15 minutes.

CHICKEN BAKED IN YOGURT

4 chicken breasts, each about 185 g (6½ oz)
4 tablespoons lemon juice
1 teaspoon salt
Marinade:
1 medium onion, peeled and coarsely chopped
2 teaspoons ground turmeric
1 garlic clove, peeled
4 slices fresh root ginger, peeled and coarsely chopped
1 tablespoon garam masala
250 ml (8 fl oz) plain unsweetened yogurt
To garnish:
chopped fresh coriander or parsley
lemon wedges

Preparation time: 15 minutes, plus marinating
Cooking time: 12 minutes
Microwave setting: Full (100%)

1. Make 3 or 4 diagonal slashes across each chicken breast and rub them on both sides with lemon juice and salt. Place them in a shallow dish and leave in a cool place for 20 minutes.
2. Place the onion, turmeric, garlic, ginger, garam masala and yogurt in a liquidizer or food processor and purée until smooth.
3. Rub the marinade into the chicken, then cover and refrigerate for 8-12 hours, turning over two or three times.
4. Place the dish in the microwave and cook, covered, for 12 minutes or until the chicken is cooked, turning the breasts over and rearranging them after 6 minutes.
5. Drain the marinade and discard. Place the chicken on a warm serving dish, sprinkle with chopped coriander or parsley and garnish with lemon wedges. Serve hot with boiled sweet potato and creamed corn.

From the left: Turkey marengo; Chicken with grapes

CURRIED FILLETS OF TURKEY

1 garlic clove, peeled and crushed
1 tablespoon olive oil
1 large onion, peeled and chopped
4 turkey breast fillets, total weight 500 g (1 ¼ lb)
15 g (½ oz) plain flour
250 ml (8 fl oz) hot chicken stock
1 dessert apple, peeled and chopped
1 tablespoon curry paste, or to taste
1 tablespoon tomato purée
1 tablespoon mango chutney
1 teaspoon lemon juice
50 g (2 oz) sultanas
salt
freshly ground black pepper
To garnish:
sliced tomatoes
slices of lemon

Preparation time: 10 minutes
Cooking time: 34 minutes
Microwave setting: Full (100%) and Defrost (30%)

1. Place the garlic, olive oil and onion in a large bowl and cook, covered, for 7 minutes. Stir, then arrange the turkey fillets over the onions. Cook, covered, for 4 minutes, rearranging once.
2. Remove the turkey fillets and stir the flour, stock, apple, curry paste, tomato purée, chutney, lemon juice and sultanas into the onion mixture and add salt and pepper to taste. Return the turkey fillets to the bowl and cook, covered, for 8 minutes, rearranging once.
3. Reduce the setting to Defrost (30%) and cook, uncovered, for 15 minutes, stirring once. Ⓕ Arrange on a warm serving dish and garnish with tomato and lemon slices. Serve hot with boiled rice, sliced bananas (tossed in lemon juice), poppadoms, a selection of chutneys and grated coconut.

Variation:
Cooked turkey pieces can be used for this recipe instead of turkey fillets. Stir them into the curry sauce and cook on Defrost (30%) for 15 minutes, stirring once.

Ⓕ Can be frozen for up to 3 months.
Ⓜ Microwave, covered, on Full (100%) for 20 minutes or until the turkey is very hot, gently separating the fillets and stirring after 10 minutes.

QUAILS IN WHITE WINE

Serves 2
75 g (3 oz) butter
4 oven ready quail
about 14 vine leaves
8 rashers streaky bacon, rinds removed
200 ml (7 fl oz) dry white wine
1 tablespoon oil
4 slices white bread, crusts removed, cut into triangles
1 tablespoon cornflour
water
salt
freshly ground black pepper

Preparation time: 15 minutes
Cooking time: 38 minutes
Microwave setting: Full (100%) and Defrost (30%), and Conventional hob

1. Place 15 g (½ oz) of the butter inside each bird, then wrap them in the vine leaves. Stretch the bacon rashers with the back of a knife and wrap two rashers round each bird. Secure with wooden cocktail sticks.
2. Place the quails, breast side down, in a large bowl and cook, covered, for 5 minutes.
3. Pour over the wine and cook, covered, for a further 5 minutes. Reduce the setting to Defrost (30%) then turn the birds over and cook, covered, for 20 minutes or until tender, turning them over again after 10 minutes.
4. Meanwhile, melt the remaining butter with the oil in a frying pan on a conventional hob and fry the bread on both sides until golden brown. Keep warm.
5. Lift the quails from the cooking liquid and remove the cocktail sticks, bacon and vine leaves. Keep the quails and bacon warm and discard the vine leaves.
6. Mix the cornflour with a little water to make a smooth paste and stir into the sauce with salt and pepper to taste. Cook for 3 minutes, stirring every 1 minute.
7. Put the fried bread on a warm serving dish and place the quails on top. Spoon over a little sauce and arrange the bacon over the quail. Serve hot with sauté potatoes, Brussels sprouts and the remaining sauce separately.

RABBIT WITH BLACK OLIVES

1 × 1 kg (2 lb) rabbit, skinned and jointed
2 tablespoons olive oil
2 garlic cloves, peeled and crushed
1 teaspoon dried rosemary
200 ml (7 fl oz) red wine
50 ml (2 fl oz) chicken stock
1 tablespoon tomato purée
2 tomatoes, skinned and chopped
salt
freshly ground black pepper
225 g (8 oz) black olives, stoned and halved

Preparation time: 20 minutes
Cooking time: 1 hour 6 minutes
Microwave setting: Full (100%) and Defrost (30%)

1. Place the rabbit joints around the base and sides of a large bowl and cook, covered, for 6 minutes.
2. Stir in the oil, garlic, rosemary, wine, stock, tomato purée, tomatoes and salt and pepper to taste. Cook, covered, for 15 minutes, then rearrange and reduce the setting to Defrost (30%). Cook, covered, for 45 minutes or until tender, rearranging every 15 minutes. Add the olives 15 minutes before the end of cooking. F
3. Arrange the rabbit and olives on a warm serving dish and pour over a little of the sauce. Serve immediately with boiled rice, braised fennel and the remaining sauce separately.

F Can be frozen for up to 3 months.
M Microwave, covered, on Full (100%) for 20 minutes or until very hot, breaking up and stirring twice.

From the left: Curried fillets of turkey; Quails in white wine

NORMANDY PHEASANT

Under no circumstances, can spirits be heated on their own in a microwave. Always heat them in a small saucepan on a conventional hob.

2 pheasants, each about 750 g (1¾ lb)
freshly ground black pepper
4 rashers back bacon
750 g (1½ lb) potatoes, peeled and quartered
3 tablespoons water
4 tablespoons Calvados, warmed
50 g (2 oz) butter
1 tablespoon oil
200 ml (7 fl oz) dry cider
450 ml (¾ pint) double cream

Preparation time: 25 minutes
Cooking time: 30-35 minutes, plus standing or browning
Microwave setting: Full (100%), and Conventional hob and oven: 200°C, 400°F, Gas Mark 6 (optional)

1. Sprinkle the inside of each pheasant with pepper. Place 2 rashers of bacon over the breast of each bird and secure with wooden cocktail sticks. Place the pheasants in roasting bags and secure with non-metallic ties, then prick the bags and place in a shallow dish. Cook for 19 minutes, turning over once.
2. Remove the pheasants from the bags and discard the bacon. Then, place the birds in a preheated conventional oven for 15 minutes until browned. Alternatively, wrap them tightly in foil and leave to stand for 15 minutes.
3. Meanwhile, place the potatoes and water in a large bowl and cook, covered, for 7 minutes. Leave to stand, covered.
4. Heat 2 tablespoons of the Calvados in a small saucepan on a conventional hob. Using a long taper set it alight and pour over the pheasants. When the flames have died down, cut the pheasants into even-sized serving pieces and keep the pieces warm.
5. Drain the potatoes. Melt the butter and oil in a frying pan on a conventional hob and fry the potatoes until golden brown. Keep warm.
6. Meanwhile, pour the cider into a saucepan and boil vigorously on a conventional hob until reduced by half. Stir in the cream, a little at a time, then simmer, stirring constantly, until glossy and reduced by half. Taste and adjust the seasoning.
7. Arrange the pheasant pieces in the centre of a warm serving dish, sprinkle with the remaining Calvados and pour over a little of the hot sauce. Serve the pheasant with the sauté potatoes, Braised red cabbage with apples (page 63) and the remaining sauce separately.

CASSEROLED PIGEON WITH PEAS

1 medium onion, peeled and chopped
1 carrot, peeled and chopped
1 celery stalk, chopped
1 garlic clove, peeled and crushed
100 g (4 oz) lean bacon, rinded and chopped
4 oven ready pigeons
50 ml (2 fl oz) dry white wine
450 ml (¾ pint) hot chicken stock
¼ teaspoon ground cinnamon
salt
freshly ground black pepper
225 g (8 oz) frozen peas
25 g (1 oz) cornflour
water
To garnish:
4 slices of lemon
4 sprigs parsley

Preparation time: 10 minutes
Cooking time: 1 hour 15 minutes
Microwave setting: Full (100%) and Defrost (30%)

1. Place the onion, carrot, celery, garlic and bacon in a large bowl and cook, covered, for 7 minutes.
2. Place the pigeons, breast side down in the bowl. Add the wine, stock, cinnamon and salt and pepper to taste. Cook, covered, for 15 minutes.
3. Turn the pigeons over, then reduce the setting to Defrost (30%) and cook for 30 minutes. Turn the pigeons over again and add the peas. Increase the setting to Full (100%) and cook for a further 20 minutes.
4. Remove the pigeons and the vegetables with a slotted spoon. Place the pigeons on a warm serving dish surrounded by the vegetables and keep warm.
5. Mix the cornflour with a little water to make a smooth paste and stir into the sauce. Cook, uncovered, on Full (100%) for 3 minutes, stirring every 1 minute.
6. Pour a little sauce over the pigeons and garnish with lemon slices and parsley sprigs. Serve hot with creamed potatoes and the remaining sauce separately.

MULLED WINE

Mulled wine can be prepared very quickly in the microwave. To make about 750 ml (1¼ pints), combine 450 ml (¾ pint) red wine, 150 ml (¼ pint) water, 150 ml (¼ pint) sweet cider, 25 g (1 oz) dark brown sugar, 4 tablespoons brandy and 1 cinnamon stick in a jug, stir well, and heat, uncovered, on Full (100%) for 4 minutes, stirring halfway through. Discard the cinnamon stick and pour into 4 tumblers. Place a fresh cinnamon stick in each one, decorate with slices of apple and serve immediately.

DUCK WITH CHERRIES

1 × 1¾ kg (4 lb) duck, trussed
1 kg (2 lb) Montmorency or Morello cherries
1 tablespoon red wine
3 tablespoons cherry brandy
1 tablespoon brandy
2 tablespoons cornflour
water
about 300 ml (½ pint) hot chicken stock or strained
duck juices, skimmed
salt
freshly ground black pepper

Preparation time: 20 minutes
Cooking time: 40-41 minutes, plus standing
Microwave setting: Full (100%)

1. Place the duck in a roasting bag, prick the bag and secure with a non-metallic tie. Place it breast side down on a trivet in a shallow dish and cook for 14 minutes. Turn the duck over and pour off any juices, then cook for a further 14 minutes. Remove the duck from the bag, wrap tightly in foil and leave to stand for 15-20 minutes.

2. Cut the duck into serving pieces then place them on a plate, cover tightly and stand the plate over a pan of hot water to keep the duck moist and hot.
3. Place the cherries and wine in a large bowl and cook, covered, for 9 minutes or until tender, stirring once. Stir in the cherry brandy and brandy and set aside, covered. Keep the sauce warm.
4. Mix the cornflour with a little water in a large jug to make a smooth paste. Stir in the hot chicken or duck stock and cook, uncovered, for 3-4 minutes, stirring every 1 minute. Taste and adjust the seasoning.
5. Arrange the duck on a warm serving dish. Remove the cherries from their sauce and spoon around the duck. Stir the sauce from the cherries into the duck stock sauce and spoon over the duck. Serve immediately with creamed potatoes and green beans.

From the left: Normandy pheasant; Duck with cherries

JUGGED HARE

Butchers with a game licence sell hares complete with their blood and liver. If you do not want to include them, omit steps 2 and 8. The dish is very good without.

Serves 4-6

1 × 1.75 kg (4 lb) hare, skinned and cut into serving pieces, with liver and blood (optional)
25 g (1 oz) butter
100 g (4 oz) smoked bacon, rinded and diced
25 g (1 oz) plain flour
2 tablespoons brandy
¼ teaspoon ground mixed spice
salt
¼ teaspoon ground cinnamon
10 pickling onions, peeled
225 g (8 oz) button mushrooms
Marinade:
4 carrots, peeled and chopped
2 medium onions, peeled and chopped
1 garlic clove, peeled and crushed
1 bay leaf
¼ teaspoon freshly ground black pepper
2 sprigs fresh parsley
½ teaspoon dried rosemary
1 litre (1¾ pints) full bodied red wine
2 tablespoons red wine vinegar (optional)
To garnish:
4-6 slices of white bread, crusts removed and cut into triangles
50 g (2 oz) butter
1 tablespoon oil
sprigs of fresh parsley

Preparation time: 15 minutes, plus marinating
Cooking time: 1 hour
Microwave setting: Full (100%), and Conventional hob

---

1. First make the marinade. Place the carrots, onions, garlic, bay leaf, pepper, parsley, rosemary and wine in a large bowl and stir well. Add the hare and leave to marinate in a cool place (not the refrigerator) for 24 hours, stirring occasionally.

2. Mix the hare's blood with the vinegar in a jug and set aside in a cool place (not the refrigerator) for 24 hours.

3. Remove the hare from the marinade, drain and dry on paper towels. Strain the marinade and discard the vegetables and herbs.

4. Place the butter and bacon in a large bowl and cook, covered, for 3 minutes. Stir in the flour, then gradually stir in the brandy and half of the strained marinade. Cook, uncovered, for 5 minutes, stirring every 1 minute.

5. Stir in the mixed spice, salt, cinnamon, onions, the hare and the remaining marinade. Cook, covered, for 30 minutes, rearranging and stirring after 15 minutes.

6. Rearrange the hare and add the mushrooms. Cook,

covered, for a further 15 minutes or until the hare is tender.

7. Meanwhile, melt the butter and oil in a frying pan on a conventional hob and fry the bread until golden brown. Keep warm.

8. Transfer the hare, bacon and vegetables to a warm serving dish and keep warm. Pour the cooking liquid into a saucepan, bring to the boil, then lower the heat and simmer gently. Chop the hare liver and stir into the blood and vinegar mixture. Stir about 4 tablespoons of the cooking liquid into the blood mixture, adding only a little at a time to prevent it coagulating. Pour this mixture slowly into the cooking liquid in the saucepan stirring constantly, then simmer gently, without boiling, for 2 minutes.

9. Pour the sauce over the hare, bacon and vegetables and garnish with the triangles of fried bread and the parsley and serve very hot with dumplings or forcemeat balls.

DUCK CASSEROLE

½ green pepper, diced
1 garlic clove, peeled and crushed
1 onion, peeled and chopped
1 carrot, peeled and sliced
1 celery stick, chopped
50 g (2 oz) butter
1 tablespoon oil
4 duck legs, each about 225 g (8 oz)
225 g (8 oz) tomatoes, skinned and chopped
50 g (2 oz) mushrooms, sliced
2 teaspoons mixed dried herbs
150 ml (¼ pint) hot chicken stock
50 ml (2 fl oz) red wine
salt
freshly ground black pepper

Preparation time: 15 minutes
Cooking time: 1 hour 18 minutes
Microwave setting: Full (100%) and Defrost (30%), and Conventional hob

1. Place the pepper, garlic, onion, carrot and celery in a large bowl and cook, covered, for 8 minutes, stirring once.
2. Meanwhile, melt the butter and oil in a frying pan on a conventional hob and fry the duck until golden brown. Drain on paper towels.
3. Add the duck to the vegetables in the bowl together with the tomatoes, mushrooms, herbs, stock and red wine and add salt and pepper to taste. Cook, covered, for 15 minutes then reduce the setting to Defrost (30%) for 55 minutes, or until the duck is tender. ꜰ
4. Remove the duck and vegetables with a slotted spoon and place on a warm serving dish. Skim the fat from the sauce and pour over the duck and vegetables. Serve hot with tagliatelle.

ꜰ The duck casserole can be frozen for up to 3 months.
ᴹ Microwave, covered, on Full (100%) for 30 minutes or until very hot. Break up and stir after 10 and 20 minutes. Continue from step 4.

TAGLIATELLE

225 g (8 oz) tagliatelle
1.75 litres (3 pints) boiling water
1 tablespoon oil
25 g (1 oz) butter, cut into pieces
65 g (2½ oz) Parmesan cheese, grated

Preparation time: 5 minutes
Cooking time: 8 minutes, plus standing

Place the tagliatelle, boiling water and oil in a large bowl and cook, covered, on Full (100%) for 8 minutes. Leave to stand, covered, for 5 minutes. Drain the tagliatelle and place in a warm serving bowl. Add the butter and grated Parmesan and toss to coat evenly. Serve immediately.

From the left: Jugged hare; Duck casserole with tagliatelle

Crown Roast with Mango Stuffing

2 best ends of neck of lamb, each with 6-7 cutlets
1 medium onion, peeled and finely chopped
25 g (1 oz) butter, cut into pieces
175 g (6 oz) mango, peeled, stoned and puréed
100 g (4 oz) fresh white breadcrumbs
1 tablespoon mixed dried herbs
25 g (1 oz) hazelnuts, finely chopped
salt
freshly ground black pepper
1 egg, lightly beaten (optional)
oil for brushing
sprigs of parsley, to garnish

Preparation time: 25 minutes
Cooking time: 29 minutes, plus standing or browning
Microwave setting: Full (100%), and Conventional oven: 190°C, 375°F, Gas Mark 5 (optional)

1. To make the crown of lamb, remove the chine bones from the best ends, make a cut across the joints about 2.5 cm (1 inch) away from the tops of the bones and scrape away all the fat and meat. Reserve the meat trimmings. Sew one end of each joint together, sewing round the last bone of each joint. Stand the joints upright and bend them round until the other ends meet. Stitch these together to form a crown.
2. Place the meat trimmings, onion and butter in a medium bowl and cook, covered, for 4 minutes. Stir in the mango, breadcrumbs, herbs, hazelnuts and salt and pepper. If necessary mix in sufficient egg to bind the mixture.
3. Place the lamb on a trivet or upturned plate in a shallow dish and brush with oil. Spoon the stuffing into the centre of the crown. Cook, uncovered, for 25 minutes, turning halfway through cooking.
4. Wrap tightly in foil and stand for 20 minutes. Alternatively, place the meat without the foil in a preheated conventional oven and cook for 15-20 minutes until it has browned.
5. Transfer to a warm serving dish and place cutlet frills on the bones. Garnish with sprigs of parsley and serve hot with vegetables in season.

Noisettes of Lamb with Maitre d'Hotel Butter

175 g (6 oz) butter
1 tablespoon finely chopped fresh parsley
salt
freshly ground black pepper
lemon juice to mix
8 noisettes of lamb

Preparation time: 10 minutes, plus chilling
Cooking time: 10-11 minutes
Microwave setting: Full (100%), and Conventional grill or hob

1. Place 100 g (4 oz) of the butter in a small bowl and microwave on Defrost (30%) for 5-10 seconds. Blend in the chopped parsley, salt, pepper and add a few drops of lemon juice to taste.
2. Place the butter on a piece of damp greaseproof paper, cover with a second piece of damp greaseproof paper and roll out until the butter is about 5 mm-1 cm (¼-½ inch) thick. Place in the refrigerator to chill and harden. Using a pastry cutter cut into 4 pieces or into 4 fancy shapes. F
3. Arrange the noisettes over the base of a shallow dish and cook, uncovered, for 7-8 minutes or until cooked, turning over and rearranging them once.
4. Melt the remaining butter in a frying pan on a conventional hob, add the noisettes and brown quickly on both sides. Or, alternatively, brown the noisettes under a preheated grill.
5. Arrange the noisettes on a warm serving dish and place a piece of maître d'hôtel butter on each. Serve with boiled new potatoes and courgettes.

F The butter can be frozen for up to 3 months. Thaw in the refrigerator for about ¾ hour before serving or use it straight from the freezer, if wished; it will start to melt once it is placed on the hot noisettes.

From the top: Crown roast with mango stuffing; Noisettes of lamb with maître d'hôtel butter

LAMB WITH APRICOTS

750 g (1 ½ lb) boned leg of lamb, cubed
½ teaspoon ground ginger
75 g (3 oz) clarified butter, cut into pieces
2 teaspoons ground coriander
1 ½ teaspoons garam masala
salt
1-2 teaspoons chilli powder
25 g (1 oz) ground almonds
300 ml (½ pint) hot lamb or chicken stock
175 g (6 oz) dried apricots, soaked overnight
25 g (1 oz) pistachio nuts
4 tablespoons double or whipping cream

Preparation time: 20 minutes, plus soaking
Cooking time: 1 hour 10 minutes
Microwave setting: Full (100%) and Defrost (30%)

1. Place the lamb, ginger, clarified butter, coriander, garam masala, salt and chilli powder in a large bowl. Cook, covered, for 10 minutes, then stir in the ground almonds and hot stock and cook for a further 10 minutes.
2. Reduce the setting to Defrost (30%) and cook for 30 minutes. Drain the apricots and stir into the mixture with the pistachio nuts. Cook for a further 20 minutes or until the meat is tender.
3. Remove the meat, apricots and nuts. Place on a warm serving dish and keep warm. Stir the cream into the sauce and pour over the meat. Serve with saffron rice.

NAVARIN OF LAMB

This dish can be very fatty. To remove excess fat, cook the navarin and leave to cool, without stirring, until the fat solidifies on the top. Lift off the fat and discard, then reheat, covered, on Full (100%) for 10 minutes.

1 celery stick, sliced
225 g (8 oz) carrots, peeled and sliced
1 small turnip, peeled and diced
1 large onion, peeled and chopped
2 garlic cloves, crushed
1 teaspoon dried rosemary
2 tablespoons tomato purée
450 ml (¾ pint) hot lamb stock
2 breasts of lamb, cut into single rib pieces
salt
freshly ground black pepper
20 g (¾ oz) cornflour
water

Preparation time: 20 minutes
Cooking time: 1 hour 23 ½ inutes
Microwave setting: Full (100%) and Defrost (30%)

1. Place the celery, carrots, turnip, onion, garlic and rosemary in a large bowl. Cook, covered, for 10 minutes, stirring once.
2. Stir in the tomato purée, stock and lamb and add salt and pepper to taste. Cook, covered, for 10 minutes, then stir.
3. Reduce the setting to Defrost (30%) and cook, covered, for 1 hour or until tender, stirring once or twice during cooking. Strain the cooking liquid and reserve.
4. Place the lamb and vegetables in a warm serving dish

LAMB IN EGG AND LEMON SAUCE

25 g (1 oz) butter
1 medium onion, peeled and finely chopped
1 celery stick, chopped
50 g (2 oz) bacon, rinded and finely chopped
1 kg (2 lb) boned shoulder of lamb, cut into 1-2 cm
(½-¾ inch) cubes
pinch of grated nutmeg
salt
freshly ground black pepper
2 tablespoons dry white wine
300 ml (½ pint) hot chicken stock
2 garlic cloves, peeled and crushed
1 tablespoon chopped fresh parsley
3 egg yolks
2 tablespoons lemon juice
25 g (1 oz) Parmesan cheese, finely grated

Preparation time: 15 minutes
Cooking time: 1 hour 1 minute
Microwave setting: Full (100%), Defrost (30%), and
Conventional hob

1. Place the butter, onion, celery and bacon in a large bowl and cook, covered, for 6 minutes.
2. Stir in the lamb, nutmeg, salt and pepper to taste, the wine, stock, garlic and parsley. Cook, covered, for 10 minutes, stirring once. Stir again, then reduce the setting to Defrost (30%) for 45 minutes or until the meat is tender. Ⓕ
3. Put the egg yolks in a bowl with the lemon juice and Parmesan cheese. Beat well to mix, then stir in a little of the hot cooking liquid.
4. Transfer the lamb mixture to a saucepan and gradually stir in the egg mixture. Cook very gently on a conventional hob, stirring constantly, until the sauce thickens. (Do not allow it to boil or the sauce will curdle.) Serve immediately with creamed potatoes and mange-touts.

Ⓕ Can be frozen for up to 3 months.
Ⓜ Microwave, covered, on Full (100%) for 30 minutes or until very hot, breaking up and stirring gently twice. Then continue from step 3.

and keep warm. Mix the cornflour with a little water to make a smooth paste and stir into the cooking liquid. Cook, uncovered, on Full (100%) for 3½ minutes or until the sauce has thickened, stirring every 1 minute. Pour over the lamb and serve immediately. Ⓕ

Ⓕ Can be frozen for up to 3 months.
Ⓜ Microwave, covered, on Full (100%) for 35 minutes or until very hot, breaking up and stirring gently twice.

From the left: Lamb with apricots; Lamb in egg and lemon sauce

TOURNEDOS PROVENCALE

1 medium onion, peeled and chopped
25 g (1 oz) button mushrooms
2 garlic cloves, peeled and crushed
2 teaspoons mixed dried herbs
25 g (1 oz) butter, cut into pieces
25 g (1 oz) plain flour
2 tablespoons tomato purée
150 ml (¼ pint) tomato juice
150 ml (¼ pint) hot beef stock
½ teaspoon sugar
salt
freshly ground black pepper
4 fillet steaks, 2.5 cm (1 inch) thick and 9-10 cm
(3½-4 inches) wide, total weight 500 g (1 ¼ lb)
fresh chervil, to garnish

Preparation time: 10 minutes
Cooking time: 12 minutes
Microwave setting: Full (100%)

1. Place the onion, mushrooms, garlic and dried herbs in a large jug and cook, covered, for 3 minutes.
2. Stir in the butter until melted, then stir in the flour, tomato purée and juice, the stock, sugar and salt and pepper to taste. Cook, uncovered, for 4 minutes, stirring every 1 minute. Keep warm.
3. Place the steaks in a shallow dish and cook, uncovered, for 5 minutes, turning over and rearranging once. Pour the cooking juices into the sauce.
4. Arrange the steaks on a warm serving platter, pour over the sauce and garnish with the fresh chervil. Serve immediately with baby Brussels sprouts and sauté potatoes.

STUFFED VINE LEAVES

Serves 4-6
225 g (8 oz) packet vine leaves in brine, drained
1 small onion, peeled and chopped
25 g (1 oz) butter
1 tablespoon tomato purée
2 garlic cloves, peeled and crushed
100 g (4 oz) long-grain rice
450 ml (¾ pint) hot lamb or chicken stock
225 g (8 oz) lean lamb, minced
salt
freshly ground black pepper
slices of lemon, to garnish

Preparation time: 35 minutes, plus soaking
Cooking time: 36 minutes, plus standing
Microwave setting: Full (100%)

1. Place the vine leaves in a shallow dish. Cover with boiling water and leave to soak for 20 minutes. Rinse the vine leaves under cold water and drain.
2. Meanwhile, place the onion, butter, tomato purée and garlic in a large bowl and cook, covered, for 4 minutes. Stir in the rice and hot stock. Cook, covered, for 9 minutes then set aside to stand, covered, for 10 minutes.
3. Place the lamb in a small bowl and cook, covered, for 3 minutes. Stir into the rice mixture. Season to taste with salt and pepper.
4. Select 20 large vine leaves for stuffing and reserve the remainder. Place the vine leaves on a flat surface, veined side upwards and put a heaped dessertspoon of the filling on to each vine leaf near to the stem. Fold first the stem end, then both sides of the leaf, over the filling and roll into a cigar shape.
5. Line the bottom of a shallow container with the remaining vine leaves and pack the stuffed vine leaves tightly over the base. Pour over sufficient hot water to cover them.
6. Cook, covered, for 20 minutes. Gently turn over halfway through cooking. Drain, place on a warm serving dish and garnish with lemon slices, if wished. Serve hot with tomato sauce and a green salad.

Variation:
Blanched cabbage leaves can be used for this recipe instead of vine leaves.

CARBONNADE OF BEEF

Serves 4-6
450 g (1 lb) onions, peeled and chopped
1 tablespoon muscovado sugar
2 tablespoons white wine vinegar
1 kg (2 lb) chuck steak, cut into 2-2.5 cm (¾-1 inch)
pieces
2 tablespoons plain flour
salt
freshly ground black pepper
1 bouquet garni
2 tablespoons made English mustard
1 crust of bread, about 1 cm (½ inch) thick
about 600 ml (1 pint) beer
4 teaspoons cornflour (optional)
water to mix
chopped fresh parsley, to garnish

Preparation time: 20 minutes
Cooking time: 1 hour 46 minutes
Microwave setting: Full (100%) and Defrost (30%)

1. Place the onion, sugar and vinegar in a large bowl and cook, covered, for 8 minutes, stirring once.
2. Stir in the meat and cook, covered, for 8 minutes. Stir in the flour, salt and pepper to taste and the bouquet garni.
3. Thickly spread the mustard over the cut side of the bread, then place the bread mustard side down on to the meat. Add enough beer to come just level with the under-

Clockwise from the top: Carbonnade of beef; Tournedos Provençale; Stuffed vine leaves

side of the bread and cook, covered, for 10 minutes. Reduce the setting to Defrost (30%) and cook for a further 1 hour 20 minutes.
4. Remove the bread and bouquet garni and discard. Season to taste with salt and pepper. F If you prefer a carbonnade with a thicker gravy, remove the meat with a slotted spoon and keep warm. Mix the cornflour with a little cold water to make a smooth paste and stir into the gravy. Cook, uncovered, on Full (100%) for 2-3 minutes, stirring once. Spoon into a deep warm serving dish and garnish with chopped parsley. Serve immediately with boiled potatoes and green peas.

F Can be frozen for up to 3 months.
M Microwave, covered, on Full (100%) for 30 minutes or until the meat is very hot, breaking up and stirring several times.

BOEUF EN DAUBE

750 g (1½ lb) lean stewing steak, cut into 2.5 cm (1 inch) cubes
100 g (4 oz) unsmoked streaky bacon, cut into small pieces
450 ml (¾ pint) red wine
450 g (1 lb) carrots, peeled and sliced
450 g (1 lb) onions, peeled and sliced
2 garlic cloves, peeled and crushed
25 g (1 oz) butter
bouquet garni
2 tablespoons tomato purée
1 tablespoon chopped fresh parsley
salt
freshly ground black pepper
20 g (¾ oz) cornflour
4 tablespoons single cream or milk
chopped fresh parsley, to garnish

Preparation time: 20 minutes, plus marinating
Cooking time: 1 hour 23 minutes
Microwave setting: Full (100%) and Defrost (30%)

1. Place the steak, bacon, wine, carrots, onions and garlic in a large bowl and leave to marinate for 3-4 hours, stirring occasionally.
2. Cook, covered, for 20 minutes, stirring once. Stir in the butter, bouquet garni, tomato purée, parsley and add salt and pepper to taste.
3. Reduce the setting to Defrost (30%) and cook, covered, for 1 hour or until the meat is tender, stirring occasionally. Remove the bouquet garni and spoon the meat and vegetables on to a warm serving dish. Keep warm.
4. Blend the cornflour and cream together to make a smooth paste and stir into the cooking liquid. Cook, uncovered, on Full (100%) for 3 minutes, stirring every 1 minute. Check and adjust the seasoning, if necessary.
5. Spoon the sauce over the meat and garnish with chopped parsley. Serve with boiled potatoes or rice.

STEAK, KIDNEY AND OYSTER PUDDING

It is most important that this pudding is served freshly made as it tends to harden on cooling.

450 g (1 lb) braising steak, cut into 2.5 cm (1 inch) cubes
150 ml (¼ pint) red wine
1 medium onion, peeled and chopped
1 teaspoon dried mixed herbs
25 g (1 oz) plain flour
salt
freshly ground black pepper
175 g (6 oz) ox kidney, cored, skinned and chopped
6-8 oysters, fresh or canned
paprika, to garnish
Suet crust pastry:
225 g (8 oz) self-raising flour
pinch of salt
4 oz shredded suet
150-200 ml (5-7 fl oz) water

Preparation time: 30 minutes, plus marinating
Cooking time: 1 hour 6 minutes
Microwave setting: Full (100%) and Defrost (30%)

1. Place the steak in a shallow bowl. Pour over the wine and marinate for 24 hours, stirring the mixture occasionally. Drain the wine from the meat and reserve to serve as gravy, if wished.
2. Place the onion and the mixed herbs in a large bowl. Cook, covered, for 4 minutes. Stir in the meat and cook for 3 minutes.
3. Stir in the flour and add salt and pepper to taste. Cook, covered, for 10 minutes, stirring after 5 minutes. Stir in the kidney and lower the setting to Defrost (30%). Cook, covered, for 40 minutes or until the meat is tender. Stir in the oysters.
4. Mix together the flour, salt and suet. Add enough water to make a dough. Roll out two-thirds of the dough and use to line a greased 1.25 litre (2 pint) pudding basin. Roll out the remainder to make a lid.
5. Spoon the meat and gravy into the lined basin. Dampen the pastry edges with water and seal on the pastry lid. Cover loosely with cling film and cook on Full (100%) for 9 minutes or until tender.
6. Remove the film. Wrap a napkin around the basin, garnish with paprika and serve immediately with boiled potatoes and buttered cabbage.

From the left: Steak, kidney and oyster pudding; Beef olives

BEEF OLIVES

4 thin slices topside of beef, about 100 g (4 oz) each
sprigs of fresh tarragon, to garnish
Stuffing:
1 small onion, peeled and quartered
1 tablespoon brandy
1 tablespoon tomato purée
1 garlic clove, peeled
3 tablespoons water
1 teaspoon chopped fresh tarragon
grated rind of 1 lemon
salt
freshly ground black pepper
50 g (2 oz) walnuts, finely chopped
25 g (1 oz) fresh white breadcrumbs
Sauce:
1 celery stick, finely chopped
100 g (4 oz) mushrooms, chopped
1 garlic clove, peeled and finely chopped
40 g (1½ oz) butter, cut into pieces
2 tablespoons plain flour
85 ml (3 fl oz) red wine
50 ml (2 fl oz) water
1 tablespoon double or whipping cream
2 teaspoons tomato purée

Preparation time: 15 minutes
Cooking time: 12 minutes
Microwave setting: Full (100%)

1. Using the jagged side of a wooden steak hammer, beat out the beef slices and set aside. To make the stuffing, place the onion, brandy, tomato purée, garlic, water, chopped tarragon, lemon rind and salt and pepper to taste in a liquidizer or food processor. Blend until smooth, then stir in the walnuts and breadcrumbs.
2. Divide the mixture between the beef slices and roll up into round parcels. Secure with string or wooden cocktail sticks. Arrange, well-spaced, in a shallow dish and cook, uncovered, for 6 minutes, turning them over once. Cover and set aside.
3. Place the finely chopped celery, chopped mushrooms and garlic in a large jug and cook, covered, for 4 minutes or until the celery is soft, stirring once. Stir in the butter until it has melted. Stir in the flour, then the wine, water, salt and pepper and the juices from the meat. Cook, uncovered, for 2 minutes.
4. Stir the cream into the sauce with the tomato purée and pour over the meat. Ⓕ Reheat if necessary, for 2 minutes. Garnish with sprigs of fresh tarragon and serve with buttered noodles.

Ⓕ Can be frozen for up to 3 months.
Ⓜ Microwave, covered, on Full (100%) for 10 minutes then gently separate the beef olives and turn them over. Cook for a further 6 minutes or until hot.

BAKED GAMMON

When cooking a gammon joint of a different weight, allow an extra 9 minutes for each 450 g (1 lb).

1 × 1¼ kg (2½ lb) middle gammon joint,
soaked overnight in cold water
2 tablespoons clear honey
3-4 tablespoons chopped fresh parsley
sprigs of parsley, to garnish

Preparation time: 10 minutes, plus soaking
Cooking time: 22 minutes, plus standing or browning
Microwave setting: Full (100%), and Conventional oven:
180°C, 350°F, Gas Mark 4 (optional)

---

1. Drain the gammon and place in a roasting bag. Close with a non-metallic tie, prick the bag and place in a shallow dish. Cook for 22 minutes, turning over once. Remove the gammon from the bag and place in a roasting tin.
2. Place the honey in a small bowl and heat for 30 seconds, then spread over the joint. Place the joint in a preheated conventional oven for 25 minutes, until browned. Alternatively, remove the joint from the roasting bag and wrap tightly in foil. Leave to stand for 25 minutes, then brush with the honey.
3. Sprinkle over the chopped parsley and, using the back of a spoon, press over the surface of the gammon. Garnish with the parsley sprigs.

ROAST PORK WITH PLUMS

Serves 6
1.5 kg (3 lb) boned loin of pork, rolled and tied
Plum sauce:
25 g (1 oz) butter
1 medium onion, peeled and sliced
2 tablespoons tomato purée
50 g (2 oz) soft dark brown sugar
1 kg (2 lb) plums, stoned
1 tablespoon cornflour
150 ml (¼ pint) dry red wine

Preparation time: 15 minutes
Cooking time: 43 minutes, plus standing or browning
Microwave setting: Full (100%), and Conventional oven:
200°C, 400°F, Gas Mark 6 (optional)

---

1. Cover the ends of the joint with a little foil, then place in a shallow dish and cook, uncovered, for 30 minutes. (Do not allow the foil to touch the cooker walls.) Remove the foil after 15 minutes.
2. Transfer the pork to a preheated conventional oven and cook for 15-20 minutes or until well browned. Alternatively, wrap the pork tightly in foil and leave to stand for 15-20 minutes.

3. Place the butter, onion, tomato purée and sugar in a large bowl and cook, covered, for 4 minutes. Stir in the plums. Blend the cornflour with the wine to make a smooth paste and stir into the plum mixture. Cook, covered, for 9 minutes, stirring once. 🅵

4. Slice the pork and arrange around the edge of a warm serving dish. Spoon some of the plums into the centre, and drizzle a little plum juice over the meat. Serve with sauté potatoes, Brussels sprouts and the remaining plums.

Variation:
Boned and rolled shoulder of pork may be used for this recipe instead of loin.

🅵 The plum sauce can be frozen for up to 3 months.
🅼 Microwave, covered, on Full (100%) for 11 minutes or until hot, breaking up and stirring twice.

PORK WITH APPLES

Serves 4-6
1 kg (2 lb) boned loin of pork, rolled and tied
1 kg (2 lb) cooking apples, peeled, cored and quartered
25 g (1 oz) butter
4 tablespoons dry cider
2 tablespoons double or whipping cream
salt
freshly ground black pepper

Preparation time: 15 minutes
Cooking time: 30-35 minutes, plus standing or browning
Microwave setting: Full (100%), and Conventional oven:
200°C, 400°F, Gas Mark 6 (optional)

1. Place a little foil over each end of the joint. (Do not allow the foil to touch the cooker walls.) Place the pork in a shallow dish, fat side uppermost. Cook, uncovered, for 20 minutes, removing the foil after 10 minutes.

2. Transfer the joint to a preheated conventional oven and cook for 10-15 minutes or until well browned. Alternatively, wrap the joint tightly in foil and leave to stand for 20 minutes before carving.

3. Meanwhile, place the apples, butter and cider in a large bowl and cook, covered, for 8 minutes, stirring once.

4. Place the pork on a warm serving platter, and arrange the apples round it. Stir the pork juices and cream into the sauce, season to taste with salt and pepper and spoon over the apples. Serve hot with roast potatoes and peas.

From the left: Baked gammon; Roast pork with plums

PORK IN MUSTARD SAUCE

750 g (1½ lb) pork fillet
seasoned flour for dusting
50 g (2 oz) butter
Mustard sauce:
40 g (1½ oz) butter
25 g (1 oz) plain flour
200 ml (7 fl oz) milk
1 tablespoon dry English mustard
85 ml (3 fl oz) dry white wine
150 ml (¼ pint) single cream
1 teaspoon caster sugar
salt
freshly ground black pepper
To garnish:
sprigs of parsley
1 hard-boiled egg yolk, sieved

Preparation time: 15 minutes
Cooking time: 16 minutes
Microwave setting: Full (100%), and Conventional hob

1. Cut the pork into 8 rounds and beat lightly to flatten. Sprinkle each side with seasoned flour. Heat the butter in a frying pan on a conventional hob. Add the pork and fry over a medium to high heat until cooked and golden brown on both sides. Set aside and keep warm.
2. To make the mustard sauce, place the butter in a large jug and cook, uncovered, for 1 minute or until melted. Stir in the flour, then gradually blend in the milk, mustard, wine, cream and sugar. Cook, uncovered, for 5 minutes, stirring every 1 minute. Season with salt and pepper.
3. Arrange the pork on a warm serving dish. Pour over some of the sauce and garnish with the parsley sprigs and hard boiled egg. Serve with sauté potatoes, Herby carrots (page 64) and the remaining sauce separately.

PORK WITH PRUNES

8 pork escalopes, total weight 450 g (1 lb)
225 g (8 oz) dried prunes, soaked overnight in
300 ml (½ pint) water
about 150 ml (¼ pint) hot or cold chicken stock
25 g (1 oz) butter
25 g (1 oz) plain flour
1 egg, lightly beaten
salt
freshly ground black pepper
1 tablespoon double or whipping cream
chopped fresh parsley, to garnish

Preparation time: 10 minutes, plus soaking
Cooking time: 21½ minutes
Microwave setting: Full (100%) and Defrost (30%)

1. Arrange the escalopes in a shallow dish, overlapping them if necessary. Cook, covered, for 3 minutes. Re-arrange, and pour over the prunes and their soaking liquid, then reduce the setting to Defrost (30%) and cook, covered, for 15 minutes.
2. Arrange the meat and prunes on a warm serving dish and keep warm. Pour the cooking liquid into a measuring jug and add sufficient stock to make up to 300 ml (½ pint).

PORK FRICASSEE WITH RED WINE AND CREAM

1 kg (2 lb) boned loin of pork, cut into 2.5 cm (1 inch)
cubes
2 large onions, peeled and sliced
2 carrots, peeled and sliced
3 garlic cloves, peeled and crushed
2 bay leaves
2 sprigs fresh thyme
400 ml (14 fl oz) red wine
2 tablespoons olive oil
8 black peppercorns
salt
2 tablespoons plain flour
100 ml (3½ fl oz) hot chicken stock
25 g (1 oz) cornflour
water
3 tablespoons double or whipping cream
1 tablespoon tomato purée
freshly ground black pepper
To garnish:
fried croûtons (optional)
chopped fresh parsley

Preparation time: 20 minutes, plus marinating
Cooking time: 1 hour 3 minutes
Microwave setting: Full (100%) and Defrost (30%)

1. Place the pork, onions, carrots, garlic, bay leaves, thyme, wine, oil, peppercorns and salt in a large bowl. Leave to marinate for 12 hours, stirring occasionally.
2. Remove the pork from the marinade, drain and dry. Strain the marinade and reserve. Discard the vegetables.
3. Place the pork in a large bowl and cook, covered, for 5 minutes, stirring once. Stir in the flour, then gradually stir in 200 ml (⅓ pint) of the marinade and the stock to cover the meat.
4. Cook, covered, for 10 minutes, stirring once. Reduce the setting to Defrost (30%) and cook, covered, for 45 minutes or until tender. Remove the meat and place on a warm serving dish, cover and keep warm.
5. Blend the cornflour with a little water to make a smooth paste and stir into the cooking liquid. Cook, uncovered, on Full (100%) for 3 minutes, stirring every 1 minute. Stir in the double cream and tomato purée and season to taste with salt and pepper. Spoon the sauce over the meat ⨍ and garnish with fried croûtons, if wished, and chopped parsley. Serve hot with boiled rice and braised celery.

⨍ Can be frozen for up to 2 months.
Ⓜ Microwave, covered, on Full (100%) for 20 minutes or until very hot, breaking up and stirring gently after 10 and 15 minutes.

From the left: Pork in mustard sauce; Pork fricassée with red wine and cream

3. Place the butter in a large jug and cook, uncovered, on Full (100%) for 1 minute or until melted. Stir in the flour, then gradually blend in the liquid. Cook, uncovered, for 2½ minutes beating well every 1 minute.
4. Beat in the egg, stir in the cream and season to taste with salt and pepper. Pour over the pork and prunes and garnish with chopped parsley.

OSSO BUCO

25 g (1 oz) butter
1 medium onion, peeled and sliced
1 garlic clove, peeled and crushed
225 g (8 oz) carrot, peeled and thinly sliced
grated rind of 1 lemon
1 tablespoon chopped fresh parsley
2 tablespoons tomato purée
350 g (12 oz) tomatoes, skinned and chopped
150 ml (¼ pint) dry white wine
salt
freshly ground black pepper
4 pieces shin of veal on the bone, about 5 cm (2 inch)
thick, total weight 1¼ kg (2½ lb)
3 teaspoons cornflour
water
parsley sprigs, to garnish

Preparation time: 15 minutes
Cooking time: 52 minutes
Microwave setting: Full (100%) and Defrost (30%)

1. Place the butter, onion, garlic, carrot, lemon rind and parsley in a large bowl and cook, covered, for 9 minutes, stirring once.
2. Stir in the tomato purée, tomatoes, wine and salt and pepper to taste. Add the veal, pushing it under the vegetables and liquid. Cook, covered, for 25 minutes.
3. Rearrange the veal, then reduce the setting to Defrost (30%) and cook, covered, for 15 minutes or until tender.
4. Remove the veal and keep it warm. Blend the cornflour with a little water to make a smooth paste and stir into the sauce. Cook, uncovered, on Full (100%) for 3 minutes, stirring every 1 minute, then pour over the veal. F Garnish with the parsley and serve hot with Risotto alla Milanese (page 59).

F Can be frozen for up to 3 months.
M Microwave, covered, on Full (100%) for 25 minutes or until the meat is very hot, gently breaking up and stirring after 15 minutes.

VEAL WITH MUSHROOMS AND CREAM

1 kg (2 lb) veal from the leg, shoulder or breast,
cut in 1-2 cm (½-¾ inch) cubes
1 medium onion, peeled and stuck with 4 cloves
1 carrot, peeled and quartered
1 celery stick, quartered
1 leek, white part only, quartered
1 bouquet garni
200 ml (⅓ pint) dry white wine
water
salt
freshly ground black pepper
175 g (6 oz) button mushrooms
3 tablespoons lemon juice
10 pickling onions, peeled
25 g (1 oz) butter
3 egg yolks
150 ml (¼ pint) double cream
freshly grated nutmeg

Preparation time: 25 minutes
Cooking time: 1 hour 7¾ minutes
Microwave setting: Full (100%) and Defrost (30%), and Conventional hob

1. Place the veal, onion, carrot, celery, leek, bouquet garni, and white wine in a large bowl and add sufficient water to cover the meat. Season with salt and pepper and cook, covered, for 15 minutes or until boiling. Skim, then reduce the setting to Defrost (30%) and cook, covered, for 45 minutes or until the veal is tender.
2. Meanwhile, place the mushrooms in a bowl and sprinkle with 1½ tablespoons of the lemon juice. Leave to soak.
3. Using a slotted spoon, transfer the veal to a warmed serving dish and keep warm. Strain the liquid into a saucepan and discard the vegetables.
4. Place the onions and butter in a medium bowl and cook, covered, for 4½ minutes. Stir in the mushrooms and the lemon juice in which they were soaking and cook, covered, for 3 minutes. Sprinkle the onions and mushrooms over the veal. Keep warm.
5. Place the egg yolks in a small bowl with 1 tablespoon of the hot veal cooking liquid. Pour 350 ml (12 fl oz) of the remaining liquid into a saucepan. Bring to the boil on a conventional hob and cook, uncovered, over a high heat until reduced to 250 ml (8 fl oz). Stir in the cream and add nutmeg to taste.
6. Whisk a ladleful of the hot sauce into the egg yolk mixture, then whisk this back into the saucepan. Whisk vigorously for 15 seconds over low heat. (Do not allow the sauce to boil at this stage or it will curdle.) Whisk in the remaining lemon juice, then taste and adjust the seasoning. Pour the sauce over the veal and serve immediately with boiled rice and fried aubergines.

VEAL ESCALOPES WITH HAM, CHEESE AND TOMATO

½ onion, peeled and finely chopped
1 tablespoon olive oil
225 g (8 oz) tomatoes, skinned and mashed
salt
freshly ground black pepper
4 veal escalopes, each about 100 g (4 oz)
plain flour, for coating
1 egg (size 1), lightly beaten
dried breadcrumbs for coating
100 g (4 oz) butter
1 tablespoon oil
4 slices prosciutto or cooked ham
4 slices Gruyère cheese
chopped fresh parsley, to garnish

Preparation time: 15 minutes
Cooking time: 15 minutes
Microwave setting: Full (100%), and Conventional hob

1. Place the onion and olive oil in a small bowl and cook, covered, for 3 minutes or until soft. Add the tomatoes and salt and pepper to taste. Cook, covered, for 2½ minutes, then set aside.
2. Meanwhile, beat out the veal escalopes and coat lightly with flour, then dip them into the egg and coat with the breadcrumbs.
3. Heat the butter and the remaining oil in a frying pan on a conventional hob, add the veal and brown quickly on both sides. Transfer to a shallow dish, overlapping the escalopes if necessary. Place a slice of ham, then a slice of cheese on each one and cook, uncovered, for 3 minutes or until the cheese has melted.
4. Reheat the sauce, uncovered, for 2 minutes or until hot, then pour over the escalopes and sprinkle with chopped parsley. Serve immediately with buttered spaghetti and mushrooms.

Clockwise from top left: Osso buco; Veal escalopes with ham, cheese and tomato; Veal with mushrooms and cream

CURRIED PARSNIP SOUP

1 tablespoon mild curry powder
1 large onion, peeled and chopped
1 stick celery, finely chopped
750 g (1½ lb) parsnips, peeled and thinly sliced
1 tablespoon white wine vinegar
25 g (1 oz) butter
15 g (½ oz) plain flour
600 ml (1 pint) milk
300 ml (½ pint) hot vegetable stock
salt
freshly ground black pepper
2 tablespoons double cream
fried croûtons, to garnish

Preparation time: 15 minutes
Cooking time: 19 minutes
Microwave setting: Full (100%)

1. Place the curry powder, onion, celery, parsnips, vinegar and butter in a large bowl and cook, covered, for 13 minutes, stirring halfway through cooking.
2. Stir in the flour, then the milk, and cook, covered, for 6 minutes, stirring halfway through cooking.
3. Add the hot stock and season to taste with salt and pepper. Place the mixture in a liquidizer or food processor and blend until the mixture is smooth. Stir in the cream. F Pour into warm bowls, garnish with croûtons and serve with hot toast.

F Can be frozen, without the croûtons, for up to 3 months.
M Microwave, uncovered, on Full (100%) for about 20 minutes, breaking up and stirring twice. Garnish before serving.

THAWING FROZEN SOUP

If a soup has been frozen in a plastic container, place it in the microwave and cook on Full (100%) for 1-3 minutes. The frozen block can then be lifted out and transferred to a more suitable one before continuing with the recipe. Soups which are to be served chilled should be removed from the microwave while they are still icy cold and left to stand until they have thawed completely. Whisking will help speed up the thawing process considerably.

TOMATO SPAGHETTI SOUP

Serves 4-6
1 × 225 g (8 oz) onion, peeled and chopped
1 × 175 g (6 oz) potato, peeled and sliced
25 g (1 oz) butter
450 g (1 lb) tomatoes, skinned and quartered
1 teaspoon dried sweet basil
750 ml (1¼ pints) hot vegetable stock
2 tablespoons tomato purée
300 ml (½ pint) milk
25 g (1 oz) spaghetti, broken into small pieces
salt
freshly ground black pepper
chopped chives or freshly chopped basil, to garnish

Preparation time: 10 minutes
Cooking time: 28 minutes
Microwave setting: Full (100%)

1. Place the onion, potato and butter in a large bowl and cook, covered, for 4 minutes.
2. Stir in the tomatoes and basil. Cook, covered, for a further 4 minutes.
3. Add 600 ml (1 pint) of the hot stock to the vegetables and purée in a liquidizer or food processor. Return to the bowl and stir in the tomato purée, milk and spaghetti. Add salt and pepper to taste.
4. Cook, uncovered, for 20 minutes or until the spaghetti is cooked. Thin the soup with the remaining stock and reheat if necessary. F Garnish with the chives or fresh basil and serve with French bread.

F This soup can be frozen for up to 3 months.
M Microwave, uncovered, on Full (100%) for about 20 minutes or until hot. Gently break up and stir after 10 and 15 minutes. Garnish before serving.

From the top: Tomato spaghetti soup; Curried parsnip soup

LETTUCE SOUP

1 large onion, peeled and chopped
25 g (1 oz) butter
225 g (8 oz) lettuce
450 ml (¾ pint) hot chicken stock
1 teaspoon dried rosemary
1 tablespoon tomato purée
salt
freshly ground black pepper
1 tablespoon cornflour
300 ml (½ pint) milk
2 tablespoons double cream
To garnish:
sprigs of fresh rosemary or chopped fresh parsley

Preparation time: 10 minutes
Cooking time: 17 minutes
Microwave setting: Full (100%)

1. Place the onion and butter in a large bowl and cook, covered, for 5 minutes. Stir in the lettuce and cook, covered, for a further 4 minutes.
2. Add the stock, then pour the mixture into a liquidizer and blend until smooth, then stir in the dried rosemary, tomato purée, and salt and pepper to taste.
3. Blend the cornflour with a little of the milk to make a smooth paste, then stir in the remaining milk and add this to the vegetable purèe.
4. Cook the soup, uncovered, for 8 minutes, stirring halfway through cooking, then stir in the cream. F Garnish with the fresh rosemary or parsley, if wished, and serve with French bread.

F This soup can be frozen without the garnish for up to 3 months.
M Microwave, uncovered, on Full (100%) for about 20 minutes or until hot, breaking up and stirring twice.

AUBERGINE CREAM POTS

This starter can also be chilled and served cold.

450 g (1 lb) aubergines
salt
75 g (3 oz) full fat soft cheese with garlic and herbs
freshly ground black pepper
50 g (2 oz) toasted or roasted cashew nuts, chopped
To garnish:
4 sprigs parsley
4 cashew nuts

Preparation time: 15 minutes, plus draining
Cooking time: 10 minutes
Microwave setting: Full (100%)

1. Cut the aubergines into thick slices. Remove the skin and discard, and roughly dice the flesh. Place in a colander, sprinkle with salt and leave to drain for about 20 minutes, then rinse off the salt with cold water.
2. Place the aubergines in a large bowl and cook, covered, for 7 minutes. Stir halfway through cooking.
3. Meanwhile, place the cheese in a medium bowl, adding salt and pepper to taste, and beat until smooth.
4. Purée the aubergines in a liquidizer or food processor, then beat them into the cheese. Stir in the nuts. Check the

GLOBE ARTICHOKES WITH GARLIC BUTTER SAUCE

To get really good results from this sauce, it is important to take the egg yolks straight from the refrigerator and to work with an electric beater.

4 globe artichokes
300 ml (½ pint) water
1 tablespoon lemon juice
Garlic butter sauce:
2 large egg yolks (size 1), taken straight from the refrigerator
about 2 tablespoons lemon juice
water
100 g (4 oz) unsalted butter, cut into 12 pieces
1-2 garlic cloves, peeled and finely chopped
salt

Preparation time: about 20 minutes
Cooking time: 24 ½ minutes, plus standing
Microwave setting: Full (100%)

1. Using scissors, snip off the points of the outer leaves of the artichokes. Cut the stalks from the bases. Rinse the artichokes and turn them upside down to drain. Pour the water and the lemon juice into a large shallow dish and cook for 4 minutes.
2. Stand the artichokes in the acidulated water and cover the dish with cling film. Cook for 20 minutes, or until the bases feel tender when pricked with a fork. Rearrange the artichokes halfway through cooking.
3. Leave to stand, covered, for 10 minutes. Drain the artichokes and leave them to cool. Remove the chokes.
4. Meanwhile, place the egg yolks and the remaining lemon juice in a small jug. Beat lightly, then cook, uncovered, for 15 seconds. Beat well and cook for a further 10-15 seconds. Continue beating until the mixture begins to thicken: if it shows signs of 'scrambling', beat in 1 teaspoon of cold water.
5. Beat in 1 piece of the butter until it is completely blended. Beat in the remaining butter, piece by piece, until all the butter has been absorbed.
6. Stir in the garlic and salt and add more lemon juice if required. Spoon the sauce into a serving bowl and hand separately. Serve immediately.

Variation:
To give the sauce a consistency more like Hollandaise sauce, microwave in the jug for 10-15 seconds after all the butter has been added, and then beat well.

seasoning, then cook, uncovered, for 3 minutes. Stir every 1 minute. ☐F
5. Pile into 4 warmed ramekin dishes and garnish each one with a sprig of parsley and a nut. Serve with hot toast.

☐F Can be frozen, without the garnish, for up to 3 months.
☐M If serving cold: microwave, uncovered, on Full (100%) for 2 minutes. Stand for 15 minutes then garnish as in step 5. If serving hot: microwave, uncovered, on Full (100%) for 6 minutes, and garnish before serving.

From the left: Lettuce soup; Globe artichokes with garlic butter sauce

TOMATO AND ANCHOVY PIZZA

If you do not have a browning dish, ignore step 5 and use a non-metallic plate and do not oil the dough.

Serves 2
Pizza dough:
50 ml (2 fl oz) milk
10 g (¼ oz) fresh yeast
pinch of caster sugar
25 g (1 oz) butter
1 egg, lightly beaten
175 g (6 oz) plain wholewheat flour, sifted with
a pinch of salt
olive oil for brushing (if using a browning dish)
Topping:
350 g (12 oz) onions, peeled and sliced
1 tablespoon olive oil
1 garlic clove, crushed
225 g (8 oz) tomatoes, skinned and chopped
1 tablespoon tomato purée
salt
freshly ground black pepper
1 × 50 g (2 oz) can anchovies, drained and chopped
2 garlic cloves, peeled and chopped
8 black olives, stoned and halved
1 tablespoon chopped fresh basil

Preparation time: 20 minutes, plus rising
Cooking time: 20 minutes, plus standing
Microwave setting: Full (100%)

1. Place the milk in a small jug and cook, uncovered, for 15 seconds. Sprinkle in the yeast and sugar and stand for 10 minutes or until the mixture is frothy. Place the butter in a small bowl and cook, uncovered, for 1 minute or until it has melted.
2. Pour the yeast mixture, butter and egg into the flour. Mix to a soft dough, then knead for 10 minutes or until smooth. Place in a lightly oiled bowl, cover and cook for 30 seconds, then stand, covered, for 10 minutes. Set the dough aside in a warm place to double in size.
3. Make the topping while the dough is proving. Place the onions, oil and garlic in a large bowl and cook, covered, for 7 minutes or until the onions are soft. Stir in the tomatoes and tomato purée, add salt and pepper to taste and cook, covered, for 5 minutes.
4. Preheat the browning dish for 4 minutes or as directed by the manufacturer.
5. Meanwhile, knead the dough and roll it out to make a 23 cm (9 inch) diameter circle. Lightly brush the top with oil and place the dough, oiled side down, into the browning dish. Cook, uncovered, for 2½ minutes.
6. Spread the onion and tomato mixture over the pizza base and arrange the anchovies, chopped garlic and olives on top. Sprinkle with the basil and cook, uncovered, for 3 minutes. Serve immediately.

SPINACH GNOCCHI

Serves 2-4
225 g (8 oz) frozen chopped spinach
175 g (6 oz) Ricotta cheese
15 g (½ oz) butter
2 eggs, lightly beaten
65 g (2½ oz) plain flour
25 g (1 oz) Parmesan cheese, finely grated
⅓ teaspoon ground nutmeg
salt
freshly ground black pepper
water

Preparation time: 25 minutes, plus chilling
Cooking time: about 30 minutes
Microwave setting: Full (100%), and Conventional hob

1. Place the frozen spinach in a small bowl and cook, uncovered, for about 4 minutes or until thawed. Then place the spinach in a fine sieve and press to extract as much water as possible; do not rub the spinach through the sieve. Discard the water.
2. Return the spinach to the bowl and cook, uncovered, for 3 minutes to draw off more moisture. Stir in the Ricotta and butter and cook, uncovered, for 2½ minutes. Stir halfway through cooking.
3. Stir in the eggs, flour, Parmesan and nutmeg. Add salt and pepper to taste, and set aside to chill for 2 hours or until firm.
4. Bring a large pan of lightly salted water to the boil on a conventional hob, then lower the heat to keep the water simmering.
5. Place spoonfuls of the gnocchi mixture on to a floured board then, with floured hands, shape them into small balls about the size of large walnuts. Drop the gnocchi into the water and, as soon as they puff up and float on the surface of the water, remove them with a slotted spoon. Each batch will take about 10 minutes.
6. Arrange the gnocchi on a warm, buttered serving dish and serve immediately. If desired, sprinkle extra Parmesan over the finished dish. Serve as a starter or as a vegetable with a hot fish, meat or poultry dish.

Variation:
Sieved cottage cheese can be used instead of Ricotta.

Clockwise from the left: Tomato and anchovy pizza; Spinach gnocchi; Ratatouille Niçoise

RATATOUILLE NICOISE

1 medium aubergine, trimmed and thinly sliced
salt
1 courgette, trimmed and sliced
6 tomatoes, skinned and chopped
1 green pepper, cored, seeded and finely chopped
1 medium onion, peeled and thinly sliced
1 tablespoon tomato purée
2 garlic cloves, peeled and crushed
6 tablespoons olive oil
sprig of thyme
freshly ground black pepper
1 tablespoon chopped fresh basil
chopped parsley, to garnish

Preparation time: about 20 minutes, plus draining
Cooking time: 15 minutes
Microwave setting: Full (100%)

1. Place the aubergine slices in a colander and sprinkle with salt. Leave to drain for 15-20 minutes to remove excess liquid, then rinse with cold water and pat dry with paper towels.
2. Place the aubergine, courgette, tomatoes, green pepper, onion, tomato purée, garlic, oil, thyme and salt and pepper to taste in a large bowl. Cook, covered, for 15 minutes, stirring after 5 and 10 minutes.
3. Stir in the basil and season to taste. F Spoon on to a warm serving dish and garnish with the parsley. Ratatouille is very versatile. It can be served hot or cold, made in small quantities for a starter or as a side dish to go with meat dishes or in large quantities for a supper dish.

F Can be frozen for up to 3 months.
M Microwave, covered, on Full (100%) for 9 minutes or until hot, breaking up and stirring twice.

SPAGHETTI WITH ANCHOVIES AND OLIVES

2-2.25 litres (3½-4 pints) boiling water
pinch of salt
1 tablespoon oil
350 g (12 oz) spaghetti
Sauce:
1 garlic clove, peeled and finely chopped
2 × 50 g (2 oz) cans anchovies, drained and chopped
1 red pepper, seeded and thinly sliced
400 g (14 oz) tomatoes, skinned and chopped
100 g (4 oz) black olives, stoned and halved
1 tablespoon capers
freshly ground black pepper

Preparation time: 15 minutes
Cooking time: 22 minutes, plus standing
Microwave setting: Full (100%)

1. Place the water, salt and oil in a large bowl. Stand the spaghetti in the water and cook, uncovered, for 1 minute to soften.
2. Gently push the remaining spaghetti under the water and cook for 9 minutes: check during cooking that all the spaghetti is completely submerged. Leave to stand, covered, for about 10-15 minutes while making the sauce.
3. Place the garlic, anchovies and red pepper in a medium bowl and cook, covered, for 4 minutes. Stir in the tomatoes, olives and capers and add pepper to taste. Cook, covered, for 8 minutes. F
4. Drain the spaghetti and pile into a warm serving bowl. Pour the sauce over the top and serve at once.

F The sauce can be frozen for up to 3 months.
M Microwave the sauce on Full (100%), covered, for 12 minutes, stirring and breaking up twice.

SPRING VEGETABLE MEDLEY

25 g (1 oz) butter
1 medium onion, peeled and finely sliced
1 small yellow pepper, seeded and finely sliced
½ head fennel, trimmed and sliced
1 medium potato, peeled and diced
1 small carrot, peeled and finely sliced
100 g (4 oz) cauliflower florets
2 garlic cloves, peeled and crushed
1 teaspoon chopped fresh parsley
1 tablespoon tomato purée
25 g (1 oz) plain flour
450 ml (¾ pint) hot chicken or vegetable stock
salt
freshly ground black pepper
sprigs of parsley, to garnish

Preparation time: 15 minutes
Cooking time: 17 minutes
Microwave setting: Full (100%)

1. Place the butter, onion, yellow pepper, fennel, potato, carrot, cauliflower, garlic, parsley and tomato purée in a large bowl, and cook, covered, for 12 minutes, stirring after 4 and 8 minutes.
2. Sprinkle over the flour and stir it into the vegetables, then gradually stir in the hot stock and salt and pepper to taste. Cook, uncovered, for 5 minutes, stirring once halfway through cooking. Garnish and serve as a supper dish.

From the left: Spaghetti with anchovies and olives; Spring vegetable medley

RISOTTO ALLA MILANESE

100 g (4 oz) butter, cut into pieces
1 small onion, peeled and chopped
3 tablespoons dry white wine
salt
freshly ground black pepper
400 g (14 oz) long-grain rice
750 ml (1¼ pints) hot beef stock
¼ teaspoon powdered saffron
100 g (4 oz) grated Parmesan cheese
4 tablespoons double or whipping cream

Preparation time: 10 minutes
Cooking time: 20 minutes, plus standing
Microwave setting: Full (100%)

1. Place 50 g (2 oz) of the butter, the onion, wine and salt and pepper to taste in a large bowl and cook, covered, for 5 minutes or until the onion is soft.
2. Stir in the rice, stock and saffron and cook, covered, for a further 15 minutes, stirring halfway through cooking. Remove from the cooker and leave to stand, covered, for 8 minutes. F
3. Stir in the remaining butter, Parmesan cheese and cream and leave to stand for 1 minute before piling into a warm serving dish.

F Freeze the rice for up to 3 months.
M Microwave, covered, on Full (100%) for 6 minutes or until hot, breaking up and stirring after 3 and 5 minutes, then continue from step 3.

COURGETTES AU GRATIN

500 g (1 ¼ lb) courgettes, trimmed and diagonally sliced
1 tablespoon olive oil
2 garlic cloves, crushed
salt
freshly ground black pepper
1 egg, lightly beaten
25 g (1 oz) fresh white breadcrumbs
25 g (1 oz) Gruyère cheese, grated

Preparation time: 10 minutes
Cooking time: 15 minutes
Microwave setting: Full (100%), and Conventional grill

1. Place the courgettes, oil and garlic in a large bowl, add salt and pepper to taste, and cook, covered, for 8 minutes, stirring halfway through cooking. Ⓕ

2. Using a fork quickly stir in the beaten egg and then transfer the mixture to a warm flameproof dish.

3. Combine the breadcrumbs and cheese and sprinkle over the courgettes. Place under a preheated conventional grill and cook until golden brown and bubbling.

Ⓕ The courgettes can be frozen after step 1. Eat within 3 months.
Ⓜ Microwave, covered, on Full (100%) for 10 minutes or until hot, gently breaking up and stirring halfway through cooking. Continue from step 2.

From the left: Courgettes au gratin; Aubergine and cheese bake; Pipérade

AUBERGINE AND CHEESE BAKE

Serves 4-6
500 g (1 ¼ lb) aubergines, trimmed and thinly sliced
salt
1 tablespoon olive oil
225 g (8 oz) onions, peeled and sliced
450 g (1 lb) tomatoes, skinned and sliced
salt
freshly ground black pepper
1 tablespoon chopped fresh basil
50 g (2 oz) Parmesan or Cheddar cheese, grated

Preparation time: 15 minutes, plus draining
Cooking time: about 25 minutes
Microwave setting: Full (100%), and Conventional grill

1. Place the aubergine slices in a colander and sprinkle them with salt. Leave to drain for 20 minutes to remove excess liquid, then rinse well in cold water and pat dry with paper towels.
2. Meanwhile, place the oil and onions in a medium bowl and cook, covered, for 6 minutes. Set aside.
3. Place 250 g (9 oz) of the aubergines in the base of a flameproof 2 litre (3½ pint) casserole dish. Spread the onions on the aubergines, then spread the tomatoes over the onions. Sprinkle with salt and pepper and 1½ teaspoons of the basil. Arrange the remaining aubergines on top and sprinkle over the remaining basil.
4. Cook, covered, for 15 minutes. Ⓕ
5. Sprinkle over the cheese and cook under a preheated conventional grill until the cheese topping is brown and bubbling. Serve as a lunch or supper dish.

Ⓕ Can be frozen without the cheese topping for up to 3 months.
Ⓜ Microwave, uncovered, on Full (100%) for 16 minutes, then leave to stand for 10 minutes. Cook for a further 10 minutes or until hot. Continue from step 5.

PIPERADE

2 large green or red peppers, halved lengthways and seeded
2 tablespoons olive oil
2 large onions, peeled and thinly sliced
½ red chilli, seeded and thinly sliced (optional)
2 garlic cloves, peeled and crushed
pinch of sugar
salt
freshly ground black pepper
450 g (1 lb) tomatoes, skinned and chopped
4 eggs, lightly beaten
4 slices ham, chopped, to garnish

Preparation time: 15 minutes
Cooking time: about 25 minutes
Microwave setting: Full (100%), and Conventional grill

1. Grill the peppers under a preheated grill until the skins are charred, then slice them into thin strips.
2. Place the peppers, oil, onions, red chilli, if using, garlic, sugar and salt and pepper to taste in a medium bowl and cook, covered, for 10 minutes, stirring halfway through cooking.
3. Stir in the tomatoes, and cook, covered, for a further 6 minutes, stirring halfway through cooking.
4. Using a fork, stir in the eggs and cook, uncovered, for 2 minutes, stirring twice.
5. Pile the pipérade mixture on to a warm serving dish and sprinkle the ham around it. Serve as a supper dish or light lunch with hot toast.

BROAD BEAN RAGOUT

1 medium onion, peeled and chopped
1 carrot, peeled and thinly sliced
2 garlic cloves, peeled and crushed
25 g (1 oz) butter
50 g (2 oz) bacon, chopped
salt
freshly ground black pepper
450 g (1 lb) frozen shelled broad beans

Preparation time: 10 minutes
Cooking time: 16 minutes, plus standing
Microwave setting: Full (100%)

1. Place the onion, carrot, garlic, butter and bacon in a large bowl and cook, covered, for 8 minutes, stirring halfway through cooking.
2. Stir in salt and pepper to taste, add the beans and cook, covered, for 8 minutes, stirring halfway through cooking. Leave, covered, for 5 minutes before spooning into a warm serving dish. F Serve with a hot fish, meat or poultry dish.

F Can be frozen for up to 1 month.
M Microwave, covered, on Full (100%) for 7 minutes, breaking up and stirring halfway through cooking. Stand, covered, for 5 minutes, then cook for a further 3 minutes.

THAWING FROZEN VEGETABLES

Frozen vegetables can be thawed very quickly in the microwave without adding any extra water. They must be covered first and frequently the Full (100%) setting can be used, but always check with the manufacturer's instructions. If there are any large lumps of ice, remove these and discard them during the thawing process. Once thawing has started, the vegetables should be separated, stirred or rearranged.

GLAZED SHALLOTS

450 g (1 lb) whole shallots, trimmed and peeled
25 g (1 oz) butter
50 g (2 oz) muscovado sugar

Preparation time: 10 minutes
Cooking time: 6 minutes, plus standing
Microwave setting: Full (100%)

1. Place the shallots, butter and sugar in a medium bowl and cook, covered, for 6 minutes, stirring after 3 minutes. Set aside, covered, for 3-4 minutes.
2. Drain the shallots and spoon them into a warm serving dish. Serve with hot fish, poultry, game or meat dishes.

Variation:
Caster sugar may be used instead of muscovado.

BRAISED RED CABBAGE WITH APPLES

25 g (1 oz) butter
1 medium onion, peeled and chopped
450 g (1 lb) red cabbage, coarsely shredded
2 cloves
250 ml (8 fl oz) hot chicken stock
salt
freshly ground black pepper
2 cooking apples, peeled, cored and sliced

Preparation time: 10 minutes
Cooking time: 17 minutes, plus standing
Microwave setting: Full (100%)

1. Place the butter and onion in a large bowl and cook, covered, for 3 minutes.
2. Stir in the cabbage, cloves and hot stock and add salt and pepper to taste. Cook, covered, for 4 minutes.
3. Stir in the apples and cook, covered, for 10 minutes, stirring halfway through cooking. F
4. Stand, covered, for 5 minutes, then drain and spoon into a warm serving dish. Serve with hot meat, poultry or game dishes.

F Can be frozen for up to 3 months.
M Microwave, covered, on Full (100%) for 12 minutes or until hot, breaking up and stirring after 5 and 10 minutes.

From the left: Broad bean ragout; Braised red cabbage with apples

Herby Carrots

3 tablespoons cold water
1 teaspoon demerara sugar
450 g (1 lb) carrots, peeled and thinly sliced
25 g (1 oz) butter, cut into pieces
1 teaspoon chopped fresh thyme
1 teaspoon chopped fresh parsley
thyme sprigs, to garnish

Preparation time: 10 minutes
Cooking time: 8 minutes
Microwave setting: Full (100%)

1. Place the water, sugar and carrots in a large bowl and cook, covered, for 8 minutes or until tender, stirring half-way through cooking.
2. Drain the liquid from the carrots and stir in the butter, thyme and parsley. F Spoon into a warm serving dish and garnish with sprigs of fresh thyme.

F Can be frozen for up to 3 months.
M Microwave, covered, on Full (100%) for 9 minutes or until hot. Break up gently and stir after 4 and 6 minutes.

Gratin Dauphinoise

40 g (1½ oz) butter
1 kg (2 lb) potatoes, peeled and thinly sliced
salt
freshly ground black pepper
grated nutmeg
1 garlic clove, peeled
150 ml (¼ pint) single cream
chopped fresh parsley, to garnish

Preparation time: 15 minutes
Cooking time: 12 minutes, plus standing
Microwave setting: Full (100%)

1. Using 15 g (½ oz) of the butter grease a 18 cm (7 inch) soufflé dish.
2. Layer the potatoes in the dish, sprinkling each layer with a little salt, pepper and nutmeg.
3. Crush the garlic into the cream and pour over the potatoes. Dot with the remaining butter and cook, covered, for 12 minutes or until tender. Stand, covered, for 5 minutes. Garnish with chopped parsley. Serve with hot fish, poultry, game or meat dishes.

LEEK AND POTATO RAGOUT

450 g (1 lb) potatoes, peeled and cut into
5 mm (¼ inch) slices
350 g (12 oz) leeks, white part only, sliced
salt
freshly ground black pepper
15 g (½ oz) butter
150 ml (¼ pint) hot vegetable or chicken stock
50 g (2 oz) Cheddar cheese, grated

Preparation time: 15 minutes
Cooking time: 20 minutes
Microwave setting: Full (100%), and Conventional grill

1. Place half the potatoes in the base of a deep 18 cm (7 inch) flameproof dish. Add a layer of leeks and cover with the remaining potatoes.
2. Sprinkle over salt and pepper to taste, dot with butter and pour over the stock. Cook, covered, for 15 minutes or until the potatoes are tender, turning the dish halfway through cooking.
3. Sprinkle over the cheese and cook under a preheated conventional grill until it is melted and bubbling.

From the left: Herby carrots; Gratin Dauphinoise; Leek and potato ragout

APPLE PANCAKES

Makes 8 pancakes
1 egg (size 1) and 1 extra yolk
300 ml (½ pint) milk
100 g (4 oz) plain flour
150 ml (¼ pint) double cream
oil, for frying
cream, to serve (optional)
Filling:
750 g (1½ lb) eating apples, peeled, cored and chopped
25 g (1 oz) sultanas
25 g (1 oz) butter
½ teaspoon ground cinnamon
50 g (2 oz) demerara sugar

Preparation time: 15 minutes
Cooking time: 27 minutes
Microwave setting: Full (100%), and Conventional hob and grill

1. Beat together the egg, egg yolk and milk. Put the flour in a mixing bowl and whisk in the egg mixture. Set aside.
2. Place the apples, sultanas, butter, cinnamon and 25 g (1 oz) of the sugar in a large bowl. Cook, covered, for 7 minutes, stirring halfway through cooking. Set aside, covered. F
3. Using a small frying pan on a conventional hob make 8 thin pancakes. F Fold each pancake in half and half again to form a fan shape.
4. Fill a pocket of each pancake with a spoonful of the apple mixture and arrange the filled pancakes in a shallow flameproof dish. Pour over the cream and sprinkle with the remaining sugar. Place under a preheated grill and cook until the sugar has melted and the topping is brown and bubbling. Serve with cream, if wished.

F The pancakes and the apple mixture can be frozen separately (interleave the unfolded pancakes with greaseproof paper before freezing).
M The pancakes: Microwave, uncovered, on Full (100%) for 4 minutes. Rearrange, and remove any which may be ready, during the process.
The apples: Microwave, uncovered, on Defrost (30%) for 12 minutes, increase to Full (100%) and cook for 4 minutes or until hot.

BLACKBERRY AND APPLE CRUMBLE

Serves 4-6
750 g (1½ lb) cooking apples, peeled, cored and sliced
350 g (12 oz) blackberries
75 g (3 oz) caster sugar
Crumble topping:
100 g (4 oz) plain flour
50 g (2 oz) muscovado sugar
75 g (3 oz) butter
cream to serve (optional)

Preparation time: 15 minutes
Cooking time: 15 minutes
Microwave setting: Full (100%)

1. Place the apples, blackberries and caster sugar in a 1.6 litre (2¾ pint) soufflé dish.
2. In a mixing bowl rub together the flour, muscovado sugar and the butter until the mixture resembles fine breadcrumbs. Sprinkle over the fruit and make two or three holes in the mixture to allow the steam to escape. Cook, uncovered, for 10 minutes, turning the dish round halfway through cooking.
3. Remove the crumble from the microwave and serve hot or cold with cream. F

F Can be frozen for up to 3 months.
M Microwave, uncovered, on Defrost (30%) for 15 minutes. Stand for 20 minutes then microwave on Full (100%) for 15 minutes.

THAWING FROZEN FRUIT

Frozen fruit can be thawed successfully on either the Full (100%) or Defrost (30%) setting. Ideally it should be partially thawed, then left to stand to complete the operation. Cover the fruit and, once thawing has started, break it up gently with a fork for quicker, more even, results. Stirring once or twice during the thawing process also helps. If the fruit is in a pouch suitable for microwave cooking, pierce it before placing it in the microwave.

From the top: Blackberry and apple crumble; Apple pancakes

CHRISTMAS PUDDING

This is a Christmas pudding which you can make right at the last minute. However should you wish to make it in advance and reheat it later, refer to the cooker manufacturer's handbook for specific instructions but do not leave the pudding unattended. Do not be tempted to put silver coins or charms in it though, as metallic objects interfere with the microwaves.

Serves 6
75 g (3 oz) shredded suet
75 g (3 oz) plain flour
1½ teaspoons mixed spice
½ teaspoon grated nutmeg
¼ teaspoon salt
50 g (2 oz) caster sugar
50 g (2 oz) muscovado sugar
40 g (1½ oz) fresh white breadcrumbs
50 g (2 oz) glacé cherries, chopped
50 g (2 oz) mixed peel
50 g (2 oz) raisins
50 g (2 oz) currants
50 g (2 oz) sultanas
75 g (3 oz) dried figs, chopped
50 g (2 oz) almonds, chopped
50 g (2 oz) apple, chopped
juice and grated rind of 1 orange
grated rind of 1 lemon
2 eggs (size 1), lightly beaten
25 ml (1 fl oz) milk
25 ml (1 fl oz) dark rum
2 teaspoons gravy browning
butter for greasing
1½ tablespoons rum

Preparation time: 15 minutes
Cooking time: 24 minutes, plus standing
Microwave setting: Full (100%) and Defrost (30%), and Conventional hob

1. In a large bowl mix together the suet, flour, spice, nutmeg, salt, caster sugar, muscovado sugar, breadcrumbs, cherries, peel, raisins, currants, sultanas, figs, almonds and apple. Stir in the orange juice, orange and lemon rinds, eggs and milk. Mix together the rum and gravy browning and stir into the mixture.
2. Spoon the pudding mixture into a 1.25 litre (2 pint) pudding basin which has been well greased with butter and make a small dip in the centre of the pudding. Cook, covered, on Defrost (30%) for 20 minutes, turning the bowl round halfway through cooking.
3. Stand the pudding, covered, for 5 minutes. Increase the power setting to Full (100%) and cook, covered, for 4 minutes. Stand, covered, for 5 minutes before turning out on to a warm serving dish.
4. To serve, place the rum in a small pan and heat gently on a conventional hob. Remove the pudding from the microwave cooker, pour over the warmed rum and ignite carefully. Alternatively decorate with a sprig of holly and artificial berries.

From the left: Christmas pudding; Crème brûlée

CREME BRULEE

350 ml (12 fl oz) double cream (taken straight
from the refrigerator)
few drops vanilla essence (optional)
4 egg yolks (size 1)
1 teaspoon cornflour
75-100 g (3-4 oz) caster sugar

Preparation time: 10 minutes, plus chilling
Cooking time: 8½ minutes
Microwave setting: Full (100%), and Conventional grill

1. Place the cream in a large jug with a few drops of vanilla essence (if wished) and cook, uncovered, for 2 minutes, stirring after 1 minute. Do not allow to boil. Set aside.
2. Place the egg yolks, cornflour and 25 g (1 oz) of the caster sugar in a medium bowl. Using a hand mixer, beat for 3 minutes on medium speed until the mixture is thick and light cream in colour but not frothy.
3. Gradually beat in the heated cream then cook, uncovered, for 1½ minutes until thick and creamy; beating every 30 seconds. Beat again on removal from the cooker to ensure that the mixture is thick.
4. Pour into 4 flameproof ramekin dishes. Chill in the refrigerator until set. F
5. Sprinkle the remaining sugar over each dish and brown until bubbling under a preheated conventional grill. Serve immediately.

F Can be frozen for up to 3 months without the topping. Thaw for 1 hour at room temperature then chill in the refrigerator for 30 minutes before continuing with step 5.

TREACLE PUDDING

Serve this pudding as soon as it is ready as it hardens on cooling.

10 g (¼ oz) butter
3 tablespoons black treacle or golden syrup
100 g (4 oz) self-raising flour
50 g (2 oz) shredded suet
50 g (2 oz) caster sugar
½ teaspoon mixed spice
1 egg, lightly beaten
2 tablespoons water
4 tablespoons milk

Preparation time: 10 minutes
Cooking time: 4 minutes, plus standing
Microwave setting: Full (100%)

1. Grease a 900 ml (1½ pint) pudding basin with the butter. Spoon the treacle or golden syrup into the base and spread a little up the sides of the basin.
2. In another bowl, mix together the flour, suet, sugar and spice, then beat in the egg, water and milk. Spoon this mixture into the pudding basin.
3. Cook, covered, for 2 minutes. Turn the basin, remove the cover and cook for a further 2 minutes.
4. Leave the pudding to stand in the basin for 4-5 minutes before turning out on to a warm serving dish. Serve immediately.

PECAN AND MAPLE SYRUP CHEESECAKE

Serves 6-8
Base:
75 g (3 oz) butter
175 g (6 oz) digestive biscuits, crushed
25 g (1 oz) golden granulated sugar
Filling:
65 g (2½ oz) caster sugar
1 tablespoon water
65 g (2½ oz) shelled pecan nuts, or 225 g (8 oz)
whole pecan nuts
350 g (12 oz) full fat soft cheese
2 eggs, lightly beaten
25 g (1 oz) cornflour
85 ml (3 fl oz) maple syrup
To decorate:
150 ml (¼ pint) double or whipping cream
shelled pecan nuts

Preparation time: 20 minutes, plus chilling
Cooking time: 11 ½ minutes
Microwave setting: Full (100%)

1. Place the butter in a small jug and cook, uncovered, for 2 minutes or until melted. Stir into the crushed biscuits and granulated sugar and spread over the base of a 23 cm (9 inch) flan dish, pressing down well with the back of a spoon until it is smooth.
2. Place the caster sugar and water in a large jug and cook, uncovered, for 2 minutes, stirring after 1 minute.
3. Stir in the nuts and cook, uncovered, for 1½ minutes, stirring every 30 seconds. Spread the nut mixture over a piece of greaseproof paper and leave it to cool. Then cover with another piece of greaseproof paper and, with a rolling pin, crush the nuts thoroughly. Set aside.
4. Place the cheese, eggs and cornflour in a medium bowl and beat well. Cook, uncovered, for 4 minutes, beating well every 1 minute.
5. Slowly beat in the maple syrup, then cook for 2 minutes, beating well every 30 seconds.
6. Stir in the crushed nut mixture and spread over the biscuit base. Chill thoroughly. F
7. To serve, decorate with double cream and pecan nuts.

F Can be frozen for up to 6 months, without the decoration.
M Microwave, uncovered, on Full (100%) for 2 minutes then reduce to Defrost (30%) for 5 minutes. Stand for 10 minutes before decorating as in step 7.

PLUM CHEESECAKE

Serves 6-8
Base:
100 g (4 oz) butter
1 tablespoon golden syrup
225 g (8 oz) digestive biscuits, crushed
Filling:
225 g (8 oz) plum purée
25 g (1 oz) caster sugar
1 tablespoon powdered gelatine
300 g (11 oz) full fat soft cheese
6 tablespoons double cream
To decorate:
150 ml (¼ pint) double or whipping cream, stiffly
whipped
2 fresh plums, stoned and quartered

Preparation time: 15 minutes, plus cooling and chilling
Cooking time: 4 ½ minutes
Microwave setting: Full (100%)

1. To make the base, put the butter in a large jug and cook, uncovered, for 1½ minutes or until it has melted. Stir in the syrup until it is well blended then mix in the crushed biscuits. Place the mixture in a deep 20 cm (8 inch) round cake tin with a removable base; using the back of a spoon, press the biscuit mixture over the base and about halfway up the sides of the tin.
2. Place the plum purée and the sugar in a large jug and cook, uncovered, for 3 minutes or until very hot. Sprinkle over the gelatine and stir well until it has dissolved. Set aside to cool.
3. Beat the cheese and cream together until smooth, then gradually beat in the plum mixture. Spoon the mixture into the biscuit crumb case and smooth over. Chill in the refrigerator. F
4. Remove the cheesecake from the dish and decorate with swirls of cream and quartered plums.

F Can be frozen, without the decoration, for up to 3 months.
M Microwave, uncovered, on Full (100%) for 2 minutes then reduce to Defrost (30%) for 7½ minutes. Leave to stand for 25 minutes and continue with step 4.

From the left: Pecan and maple syrup cheesecake; Pineapple and Kirsch upside down pudding

PINEAPPLE AND KIRSCH UPSIDE DOWN PUDDING

Serve this pudding as soon as it is cooked as it tends to harden on cooling.

Fruit base:
2-3 slices fresh pineapple, 5 mm (¼ inch) thick, 1 slice left whole, the others quartered
5 tablespoons Kirsch
40 g (1½ oz) butter
25 g (1 oz) soft brown sugar
3 glacé cherries, quartered
Cake mixture:
100 g (4 oz) butter
100 g (4 oz) caster sugar
2 eggs, lightly beaten
100 g (4 oz) self-raising flour
2 tablespoons Kirsch

*Preparation time: 12 minutes, plus marinating
Cooking time: 7½ minutes, plus standing
Microwave setting: Full (100%)*

1. Place the pineapple on a plate and sprinkle over 3 tablespoons of the Kirsch. Leave to marinate for 3 hours.
2. Place the butter in a 1.25 litre (2 pint) soufflé dish. Sprinkle over the brown sugar, then cook, uncovered, for 1 minute. Arrange the pineapple and cherries over the base in a decorative pattern.
3. Prepare the cake mixture. Beat together the butter and caster sugar until light and fluffy. Beat in the eggs, fold in the flour and then the Kirsch. Gently spread the cake mixture over the pineapple base, being careful not to disturb the pattern.
4. Cook, uncovered, for 6½ minutes, turning the dish round halfway through cooking. Remove from the cooker and stand for 3 minutes before turning out. During the standing time, prick the cake mixture with a skewer and sprinkle over the remaining Kirsch. F
5. Turn out on to a warm serving dish and serve hot or warm with cream.

F Can be frozen for up to 3 months.
M Microwave, uncovered, on Full (100%) for 4 minutes or until warm to the touch. Serve at once.

CREAMY APPLE FLAN

Flan case:
100 g (4 oz) butter
1 tablespoon golden syrup
200 g (7 oz) ginger biscuits, crushed
50 g (2 oz) hazelnuts, finely chopped
Filling:
500 g (1¼ lb) dessert apples, peeled, cored and sliced
2 tablespoons lemon juice
85 ml (3 fl oz) double or whipping cream
2 eggs (size 1)
50 g (2 oz) caster sugar
¼ teaspoon ground cinnamon
To decorate:
1 red apple, cored, sliced and dipped in lemon juice
whipped cream (optional)

Preparation time: 18 minutes, plus chilling
Cooking time: 11 minutes
Microwave setting: Full (100%)

1. Place the butter in a large jug and cook, uncovered, for 1½ minutes or until it has melted. Stir in the syrup until well blended, then mix in the crushed biscuits and nuts. To make the case, take a deep 20 cm (8 inch) cake tin with a removable base and using the back of a spoon press the biscuit mixture over the base and about halfway up the sides of the tin.
2. Place the apples and lemon juice in a large bowl and cook, covered, for 7 minutes, stirring halfway through cooking.
3. Beat together the cream, eggs, sugar and cinnamon. Mix with the apples and blend in a liquidizer.
4. Return the apple and cream mixture to the bowl and cook, uncovered, for 2½ minutes, stirring every 30 seconds to avoid curdling.
5. Pour the mixture into the flan case and chill in the refrigerator. F Decorate with slices of apple and serve with whipped cream, if wished.

F Can be frozen, undecorated, for up to 3 months.
M Microwave on Full (100%), uncovered, for 3 minutes then stand for 25 minutes. Decorate before serving.

POIRES BELLE HELENE

4 dessert pears, total weight 450 g (1 lb), peeled, with
stalks left on
Sauce:
100 g (4 oz) plain chocolate, broken into pieces
3 tablespoons golden syrup
2 tablespoons double cream
1 tablespoon sherry
1-2 tablespoons single cream or milk (optional)

Preparation time: 15 minutes
Cooking time: 8½ minutes
Microwave setting: Full (100%)

1. Stand the pears on a plate and cook, uncovered, for 5 minutes or until tender. Set aside to cool. F
2. Place the chocolate in a small jug and cook, uncovered, for 3½ minutes or until it is soft and melted. Stir well until smooth then stir in the golden syrup, the double cream and the sherry. Set aside until cool.
3. Transfer the pears to a serving dish and spoon the

chocolate sauce over them just before serving. Should the sauce require thinning, stir in 1-2 tablespoons of single cream or milk.

F Freeze the pears, without the sauce, for up to 1 month.
M Cook, covered, on Defrost (30%) for 7 minutes, stand for 10-15 minutes, then continue as from step 2.

CRÈME CARAMEL

Serves 6
Caramel:
100 g (4 oz) granulated sugar
4 tablespoons cold water
Custard:
450 ml (¾ pint) milk
150 ml (¼ pint) single cream
25 g (1 oz) caster sugar
4 eggs (size 1), lightly beaten
fresh fruit, to decorate

Preparation time: 10 minutes
Cooking time: 25½-28½ minutes
Microwave setting: Full (100%) and Defrost (30%)

1. Place the sugar and water in a small bowl and cook, uncovered, for 2½ minutes. Stir well to dissolve the sugar then cook, uncovered, for a further 5 minutes or until the mixture is a golden colour. Divide this mixture between 6 ramekins and swirl around with the caramel.
2. Place the milk and cream in a large jug and cook, uncovered, for 4 minutes. Whisk in the sugar and eggs, then strain and pour the mixture over the caramel. Reduce to Defrost (30%) and cook, uncovered, for 14-17 minutes or until the custards are set, rearranging halfway through cooking. Set aside to cool, then unmould on to individual serving plates and decorate with fresh fruit. The actual cooking time will vary according to the temperature of the heated milk, so check after about 14 minutes and remove any custards as soon as they are cooked.

From the left: Creamy apple flan; Crème caramel

ORANGE BAVAROIS

2 tablespoons Cointreau
1 tablespoon powdered gelatine
300 ml (½ pint) fresh orange juice
grated rind of 1 orange
2 egg yolks
25 g (1 oz) sugar
200 ml (7 fl oz) double cream, stiffly whipped
thin strands of orange rind, to decorate

Preparation time: 15 minutes, plus chilling
Cooking time: 5 ½ minutes
Microwave setting: Full (100%)

1. Place the Cointreau in a small cup, sprinkle over the gelatine and set aside to soak.
2. Place the orange juice in a small jug and cook, uncovered, for 3 minutes.
3. Place the egg yolks in a medium bowl, add the sugar and beat until thick and creamy.
4. Gradually beat the hot orange juice and the grated orange rind into the egg mixture. Cook, uncovered, for 2½ minutes or until it has thickened slightly, beating every 30 seconds.
5. Beat in the gelatine and stir until dissolved. Set aside until it begins to set, stirring occasionally.
6. Fold in the cream and pour the mixture into a 600 ml (1 pint) mould and chill in the refrigerator until set. F Turn out and decorate with the orange strands.

F Can be frozen, undecorated, for up to 1 month.
M Microwave, uncovered, on Defrost (30%) for 6 minutes, then stand at room temperature for 1½ hours.

REDBERRY SUMMER PUDDING

Serves 4-6
1 red dessert apple, weighing 100 g (4 oz), chopped
225 g (8 oz) redcurrants
175 g (6 oz) loganberries
175 g (6 oz) strawberries
100 g (4 oz) caster sugar
9-10 slices white bread, about 5 mm (¼ inch) thick,
crusts removed
50 ml (2 fl oz) cherry brandy
To decorate:
150 ml (¼ pint) double or whipping cream
fresh redcurrants

Preparation time: 15 minutes, plus chilling
Cooking time: 7 minutes
Microwave setting: Full (100%)

1. Place the apple, redcurrants, loganberries, strawberries and sugar in a medium bowl. Cook, covered, for 7 minutes, stirring halfway through cooking.
2. Line the base and sides of a 1.25 litre (2 pint) pudding basin with the bread, ensuring that the slices overlap. Spoon in the fruit, reserving the juice, and sprinkle with 25 ml (1 fl oz) of the cherry brandy.
3. Cover the fruit with slices of bread. Spoon over some of the juice so that it colours the bread and retain any remaining juice. Place a saucer on top of the bread and put a weight on the top. Chill in the refrigerator for 24 hours.
4. Turn out the pudding on to a serving dish. Stir the remaining cherry brandy into the reserved juice and spoon over the pudding, making sure that all the bread is evenly coloured. F Decorate with whipped cream and redcurrants.

F Can be frozen for up to 3 months without the decoration.
M Microwave, uncovered, on Defrost (30%) for 6 minutes. Stand for 1½ hours or until thawed.

COLD RASPBERRY SOUFFLE

1 tablespoon sweet sherry
2 tablespoons orange juice
150 ml (¼ pint) raspberry purée
1 tablespoon powdered gelatine
2 teaspoons lemon juice
50 g (2 oz) icing sugar, sifted
150 ml (¼ pint) double cream, stiffly whipped
3 egg whites (size 1), stiffly whisked
8 fresh raspberries, to decorate

Preparation time: 15 minutes, plus chilling
Cooking time: 30 seconds
Microwave setting: Full (100%)

1. Place the sherry, orange juice and raspberry purée in a small jug and cook, uncovered, for 30 seconds or until hot. Sprinkle over the gelatine and stir thoroughly to dissolve. Stir in the lemon juice and sugar. Allow to cool, stirring once or twice during cooling. Transfer the mixture to a medium bowl.
2. Gently fold the cream, and then the egg whites, into the raspberry mixture.
3. Tie greaseproof paper around the outside of 4 individual ramekin dishes so that it extends 1.5 cm (½ inch) above the rims. Spoon the mixture into the dishes and chill until set. F
4. Remove the paper and decorate each soufflé with whipped cream and 2 raspberries. Serve with langue du chat biscuits if liked.

F Can be frozen for up to 3 months. Thaw at room temperature for about 2 hours, then decorate and serve.

Clockwise from top left: Orange bavarois; Cold raspberry soufflé; Redberry summer pudding

CARAMELIZED ORANGES

Serves 4-6
4 large oranges
175 g (6 oz) golden granulated sugar
50 ml (2 fl oz) unsweetened orange juice
120 ml (4 fl oz) water
2 tablespoons Cointreau

Preparation time: 15 minutes, plus chilling
Cooking time: 8 minutes
Microwave setting: Full (100%)

1. Using a zester, remove the rind from 1 of the oranges and place it with the sugar, orange juice and water in a medium bowl. Cook, uncovered, for 8 minutes, stirring halfway through cooking to ensure that the sugar has dissolved.
2. Peel all 4 oranges, cut into 5 mm (¼ inch) thick slices and remove any pips. Arrange on a serving dish.
3. Stir the Cointreau into the orange sauce and pour over the oranges. Chill in the refrigerator for at least 2 hours before serving. F

F Can be frozen for up to 3 months.
M Microwave, uncovered, on Defrost (30%) for 12 minutes, gently separating the orange slices after about 9 minutes. Stand for 30 minutes before serving.

TOASTED ALMOND ICE CREAM

Serves 4-6
300 ml (½ pint) milk
1 egg (size 1), plus 2 extra yolks (size 1)
300 ml (½ pint) double cream, stiffly whipped
1 teaspoon almond essence
50 g (2 oz) toasted split almonds, chopped
25 g (1 oz) toasted split almonds, cut into slivers, to decorate

Preparation time: 15 minutes, plus cooling and freezing
Cooking time: 5½ minutes
Microwave setting: Full (100%)

1. Place the milk in a small jug and cook, uncovered, for 3 minutes or until boiling. Set aside for 10 minutes.
2. Place the egg and the extra yolks in a medium bowl and beat until pale and creamy. Stir in the milk and cook, uncovered, for 2½ minutes or until the custard has thickened: beat every 30 seconds to avoid curdling.
3. Whisk the custard well, then set it aside to cool: whisk occasionally while it is cooling. Fold the cream into the cooled custard and stir in the almond essence. Transfer to a freezer container and chill in the freezer for about 1-1½ hours until it is partially frozen.
4. Whisk the ice cream mixture until it is smooth. Fold in the chopped almonds and return to the freezer until frozen. F Serve the ice cream in scoops in individual bowls. Decorate with the slivers of almond.

F Can be frozen for up to 3 months.
M Remove the ice cream from the freezer 10-15 minutes before it is required. Decorate before serving.

PEARS IN RED WINE

The pears look more attractive standing upright, but if this is not possible, lie them on their sides and turn them over at the end of step 3.

600 ml (1 pint) red wine
175 g (6 oz) caster sugar
1 lemon, sliced
4 firm dessert pears, total weight about
500 g (1¼ lb), peeled
1 tablespoon arrowroot
water
split almonds, to decorate (optional)

Preparation time: 15 minutes
Cooking time: 25 minutes
Microwave setting: Full (100%)

1. Place the wine, sugar and lemon in a large jug and cook, uncovered, for 5 minutes. Stir well to dissolve the sugar.
2. Cut a slice from the base of each pear so that it can stand upright and place all the pears in a medium bowl. Cook, covered, for 3 minutes.
3. Pour over the heated wine mixture and cook, covered, for 4 minutes. Remove the cover and turn the pears around.
4. Continue cooking, uncovered, for a further 10 minutes or until the pears are tender: this will depend on their variety and degree of ripeness. Remove the pears gently with a slotted spoon and stand them to cool on a wire rack with a plate underneath.
5. Blend the arrowroot with a little water to make a smooth paste and stir this into the wine mixture. Cook for 3 minutes, stirring every 1 minute. Set aside to cool. F
6. When both the pears and the sauce are cool, coat each pear with sauce and decorate with split almonds, if liked. Place in individual glass dishes into each of which a little sauce has been poured. Chill in the refrigerator.

Variation:
If you prefer brown pears to pink, use molasses sugar instead of caster sugar.

Clockwise from top left: Caramelized oranges; Pears in red wine; Toasted almond ice cream

CHOCOLATE CAKE

Makes one 18 cm (7 inch) cake
175 g (6 oz) soft margarine
175 g (6 oz) caster sugar
40 g (1½ oz) cocoa powder
1 teaspoon baking powder
150 g (5 oz) self-raising flour
1 tablespoon brandy
2 tablespoons milk
3 eggs (size 1)
To decorate:
300 ml (½ pint) double or whipping cream, whipped
1 tablespoon brandy (optional)
75 g (3 oz) chocolate, grated or shaved

Preparation time: 10 minutes
Cooking time: 7 minutes, plus standing
Microwave setting: Full (100%)

1. Place all the ingredients for the cake in a large bowl. Beat well until the mixture is smooth, but do not overbeat.
2. Lightly grease an 18 cm (7 inch) round cake dish, 9 cm (3½ inches) deep and line the base with lightly greased greaseproof paper. Spoon the mixture into the dish and stand it on an upturned plate and cook for 7 minutes, turning it round once or twice during cooking.
3. Leave the cake to stand for 5 minutes before turning it out, upside down (so that the bottom is now the top) on to a wire tray. Leave to cool.
4. When the cake is completely cold, whip the cream and stir in the brandy, if using. Split the cake in 2 horizontally and spread some of the cream over the bottom half. Replace the top and decorate with more whipped cream and grated chocolate chocolate shavings or shapes.

CHOCOLATE MOUSSE WITH GRAND MARNIER

Serves 4-6
225 g (8 oz) dark chocolate, broken into pieces
25 g (1 oz) butter
2 tablespoons Grand Marnier
4 egg yolks
4 egg whites, stiffly whisked
To decorate:
150 ml (¼ pint) double cream
2 tablespoons Grand Marnier

Preparation time: 10 minutes, plus chilling
Cooking time: 3 minutes
Microwave setting: Full (100%)

---

1. Place the chocolate in a medium bowl and cook, uncovered, for 3 minutes or until melted. Stir every 1 minute.
2. Add the butter, Grand Marnier and egg yolks and beat them together until the mixture is smooth.
3. Gently fold in the egg whites and spoon into a 1 litre (1¾ pint) serving dish. Chill in the refrigerator until set. Ⓕ
4. Whip the cream until it is thick then gently fold in the Grand Marnier. Pipe the cream on to the mousse.

Variations:
Use another orange flavoured liqueur, brandy or strong black coffee instead of the Grand Marnier.

Ⓕ Can be frozen for up to 3 months.
Ⓜ Microwave, uncovered, on Defrost (30%) for 5 minutes, then stand at room temperature for 30 minutes. Decorate before serving.

COFFEE CREAMS

Serves 4-6
300 ml (½ pint) milk
2 egg yolks (size 1), lightly beaten
50 ml (2 fl oz) water
25 g (1 oz) powdered gelatine
65 g (2½ oz) caster sugar
150 ml (¼ pint) double cream
150 ml (¼ pint) whipping cream
1½ tablespoons coffee essence
To decorate:
85 ml (3 fl oz) whipping cream, whipped
cocoa, coffee or chocolate powder

Preparation time: 10 minutes, plus chilling
Cooking time: 5½ minutes
Microwave setting: Full (100%)

---

1. Place the milk in a large jug and cook, uncovered, for 3 minutes or until very hot. Beat in the egg yolks and cook, uncovered, for 1 minute or until the mixture starts to thicken. Beat halfway through cooking and be careful not to let the mixture curdle.
2. Place the water in a small jug and cook, uncovered, for 1½ minutes or until very hot. Stir in the gelatine until it is completely dissolved.
3. Beat the gelatine liquid and the sugar into the milk. Set aside until cool, stirring occasionally.
4. Beat the double and whipping creams together until thick and fold in the coffee essence. Check the flavour, adding more coffee essence if desired. Fold the cream into the cooled custard and pour into stemmed glasses. Chill in the refrigerator.
5. Pipe a decoration on each glass with the whipped cream and sprinkle over a little cocoa, coffee or chocolate powder. Serve with langue du chat biscuits.

From the left: Chocolate cake; Coffee creams

INDEX